Living in the Light of Death

LIVING
IN THE LIGHT
OF DEATH

On the Art of Being Truly Alive

Larry Rosenberg

with David Guy

SHAMBHALA
Boston & London
2000

Shambhala Publications, Inc.
Horticultural Hall
300 Massachusetts Avenue
Boston, Massachusetts 02115
www.shambhala.com

9 8 7 6 5 4 3 2 1

FIRST EDITION
Printed in the United States of America
∞ This edition is printed on acid-free paper that meets the
American National Standards Institute z39.48 Standard.
Distributed in the United States by Random House, Inc.,
and in Canada by Random House of Canada Ltd

LIBRARY OF CONGRESS CATALOGUING-IN-PUBLICATION DATA
Rosenberg, Larry.
Living in the light of death: on the art of being truly alive/
Larry Rosenberg with David Guy
p. cm.
Includes bibliographical references.
ISBN 1-57062-425-9 (cloth)
1. Spiritual life – Buddhism. 2. Aging – Religious aspects –
Buddhism. 3. Buddhism – Doctrines. I. Guy, David. II. Title.
BQ5395.R67   2000
294.3'444 – dc21
99-058716

Three people very dear to me died before the completion of this book. My parents, Nathan and Anna Rosenberg; and my stepdaughter, Irina Moyseev. I dedicate any merit that may arise from this text to them. May it be of some benefit in their journey.

One purpose of our practice is to enjoy our old age. But we can't fool ourselves. Only sincere practice will work.

— Shunryu Suzuki Roshi

Make good medicine from the suffering of sickness.

— Kyong Ho

One learns the art of dying by learning the art of living: how to become master of the present moment.

— S. N. Goenka

It is usually proclaimed eloquently that birth, aging, and death are suffering. But birth is not suffering, aging is not suffering, death is not suffering where there is not attachment to "my birth," "my aging," "my death." At the moment, we are grasping at birth, aging, pain, and death as "ours." If we don't grasp, they are not suffering, they are only bodily changes.

— Ajaan Buddhadasa

CONTENTS

ACKNOWLEDGMENTS

In the Buddha's teaching, everything is a dependent arising: If something appears, it is due to certain causes and conditions. This book is no exception. So many things had to come together for it to happen. I will mention only a few.

More than twenty-five years ago, J. Krishnamurti and Vimala Thakar taught me that learning how to live and learning how to die were inseparable. In fact, they are the same thing. They started me off on the right foot, and I am grateful.

My editor at Shambhala Publications, Dave O'Neal, was present at a series of talks that I gave on death awareness some years ago at the Cambridge Insight Meditation Center. He introduced himself and confidently informed me that the talks could easily be the basis for a book of some use to meditators. He then brilliantly helped the manuscript assume its present form.

My dear friend Jacalyn Bennett constantly encouraged me to turn these oral teachings into book form. She also, in a most gracious and unassuming manner, provided the financial support necessary to complete this project.

Yogis at the Cambridge Insight Meditation Center devoted many hours of their time to the accurate transcription of all my talks on death awareness. David Guy took this massive amount of material and artfully shaped it into a working document, maintaining with great sensitivity the spirit of the original talks. My wife, Galina, in her characteristically humorous and affectionate way, helped me know when to leave the computer and when to start in again. She was of immense help.

A NOTE ON TERMINOLOGY

Words from the Pali language used in the text are defined where they are used and in the glossary. But a few Mahayana Sanskrit words have become so familiar to readers of Buddhist books in the English language that we have used the Sanksrit for those words rather than the Pali. We therefore refer to a *sutra* rather than a *sutta*, to the *dharma* rather than the *dhamma*, and to *karma* rather than to *kamma*.

LIVING IN THE LIGHT OF DEATH

INTRODUCTION
Aging and Death,
Our Lifelong Companions

Aging, illness and death are treasures for those who understand them. They're Noble Truths, Noble Treasures. If they were people, I'd bow down to their feet every day.

— AJAAN LEE

MY MOST memorable learning experience about aging took place when I myself was still rather young, in my early thirties. I had been through college and graduate school and had become an academic. I had encountered a surprising amount of disappointment with that profession, perhaps because I'd expected so much from it.

At that point I had the good fortune to meet my first spiritual teacher, J. Krishnamurti, and began discovering that my true interests were in abandoning my success ethic and getting sane. I began to search inwardly and had some powerful experiences that changed how I viewed exclusively intellectual work.

Krishnamurti is famous for saying that truth is a pathless

way, but I soon realized that I needed a path, and a discipline. I began by studying yoga, which had great appeal to me. One summer I was at an ashram in Canada, attending a yoga camp, when I met an elderly man who would be very important in teaching me how to live, and age, gracefully.

His name was Shivananda Saraswati, and he was eighty-six years old, though he certainly didn't look it. He had an extremely dignified bearing, a beautiful complexion, and tremendous energy. He wasn't a teacher at the camp, though he showed us a few yoga postures. He actually lived in India, somewhere near the Himalayas, and was a lifelong monk, a teacher of Vedanta, which was a Hindu discipline. He had four students in North America, whom he taught by correspondence for many years, and they had pooled their money and paid for him to come over. He was traveling around to see them. One of the students was Canadian, which was how Shivananda Saraswati happened to be at the ashram.

He seemed more interesting than the other teachers there, so I began spending most of my time with him. Finally I decided to travel with him. He obviously had a great deal to teach me. We traveled by Greyhound bus, stopping at private residences, and I served as his attendant. I got to know him quite well.

I hadn't done much meditating at that point, but he was a fierce meditator. At 2:00 or 3:00 in the morning, no matter when we had gone to bed, he would sit up and start meditating. He didn't even wash up first. He would sit for a couple of hours right there in bed, then open his eyes quite matter-of-factly, start talking and joking, and get ready for his day.

Introduction

Saraswati had become a monk as a young man, in this Hindu tradition of Vedanta, and had been surrounded by men who took spiritual practice very seriously. They thought that getting free was the only important thing in life, and saw their bodies as obstacles to spiritual development. However, Saraswati noticed that they got ill quite frequently, which made their journey more difficult.

That hadn't seemed right to him, so he began studying hatha yoga, proper breathing, and diet. He wasn't abandoning his life as a monk; he just thought that taking care of the body enabled him to practice more effectively.

He was actually practicing, and teaching, a middle way: Don't get so obsessed with meditating that you neglect the body, and don't get so obsessed with the body that you ignore what is really important. He wasn't foolish; he knew there were no guarantees where the body was concerned. But what he said – and I have never forgotten these words – was, "If you take care of your body, and come to understand it, you may have a relatively painless old age."

He didn't mean that old age would be the same as when you were young; of course his powers weren't what they'd been twenty or thirty years before. But his old age was *relatively* painless, in stark contrast to the old people I'd grown up around. And he said that some of his deepest spiritual realizations had come after the age of seventy. Many of his desires had naturally fallen away, and he still had plenty of energy. That in itself seemed a good reason to take care of one's health.

In his teaching the Buddha emphasized the view that acquiring a human form is a rare event and an ideal one for spiritual development. There are higher realms so blissful that there isn't much motivation to practice. There are hell realms so dreadful that they overwhelm the energy to practice. But human existence is an ideal mix of bliss and suffering. It makes perfect sense to try to embody this form for as long as possible, as long as we don't become obsessed with longevity.

Shivananda Saraswati taught me a great deal about taking care of what he constantly referred to as "the" (as opposed to "my") body. Most basically he taught me that such care is an awareness practice. He didn't have a long list of rules, just lived his life and saw what effect things had on him. He saw what it was like to eat too much, and to eat too little; to take too many liquids, and not to take enough; to sleep too much, not to sleep enough; which foods helped the mind be more alert, which made it more agitated or dull. He watched the effects of various actions on his physical well-being and his mental clarity. He was extremely clean and followed yogic practices for cleansing the body, but he never saw them as a chore. He took joy in them.

All that wasn't much different from what Krishnamurti said. Our life isn't divided up into practice and nonpractice, caring for the body and caring for the mind. It is one seamless web, and awareness is the key. Krishnamurti himself, when speaking of physical health, used the metaphor of a cavalry officer and his horse. Obviously, if you're going to be riding this animal into battle, you'll want to take care of it. Your life might depend on it. It is in that spirit that you care for your body. "Your physical body may not be who you really are," Krishnamurti used to say, "but just try living well without caring for it."

From the time I was a child, growing up first in New York's Lower East Side, then Brooklyn, I had been interested in old people and the subject of aging. I'm not sure why. My grandparents lived with us when I was a child, and I loved them; my grandmother was a particular favorite. I was actually surrounded by old people in my Brooklyn neighborhood, but they were not a particularly happy group. They seemed weary and bitter, often impatient. They tempered those qualities, fortunately, with a wonderfully absurd sense of humor.

It was primarily a community of Russian Jews that I lived in, though there were some Italian immigrants around and some working-class Irish. The three groups lived in mutual disharmony. In the Jewish community the talk among the elderly was very often about health, or – more specifically – the lack of it. There were endless discussions of illnesses and medicines and operations and whether the cures were taking effect. We heard blow-by-blow accounts of the minutest changes. It was quite remarkable, sometimes more detail than you would have gotten from a medical student. But all that talk of illness wasn't especially enjoyable for a child.

My friend and I used to play a game on the boardwalk in Coney Island. We would walk along listening to old people who passed us, picking up snatches of their talk, and would make it into one huge conversation. It was easy, because so often what we heard were complaints, which we strung together into one long bitter lament. A great deal of it related to old age and illness.

Every now and then, though, I would meet exceptions to the rule, and they really seemed to stand out. People who were old, and showed signs of age, but nevertheless seemed content with their lot, bright eyed and cheerful, full of life. I really focused on such people who were aging gracefully. I wondered what their secret was.

I loved baseball in those days and was very taken with the manager of the Philadelphia Athletics, Connie Mack. The ballplayers seemed to be a crude bunch, loud and excitable, foulmouthed, but there in the middle of the A's dugout, wearing a three-piece suit, was this extraordinarily dignified man, who must have been well up in his eighties. He would disagree with the umpires like any other manager, but while the others came roaring out of the dugout kicking dirt and screaming, he would step out in a dignified way, speak his piece – losing the argument, of course – then make his way back. I forgot all about baseball when he came on the field, and watched in fascination.

I didn't have any memorable encounters with death when I was young, and in fact was shielded from it. I had my first real confrontations with death when I was in the army. I wasn't an overly enthusiastic member of the armed forces – I'd had to be drafted – but once drafted I was quite willing to serve. When I got into basic training I found, somewhat to my surprise, that I enjoyed it. I'd been an athlete when I was young, and I loved the physical rigor. I even felt the power and excitement of firing a machine gun, the kind that rested on a tripod and was handled by two people. It was exhilarating. It was like playing soldier as a child again.

But I soon discovered that we weren't playing games. When we went out on maneuvers in Germany, we were told to pitch our tents in the deep thickets of the forest. Because there weren't many good roads where we were, trucks often came through, and you didn't want to be in their way. One night after we'd gone to bed, we heard an absolutely terrifying scream. A couple of our fellow soldiers had not pitched their tent deep enough in the woods and a truck had come through and run over it. One of the men was killed instantly, and the other went psychotic. We never saw him again.

I had to face the fact that we weren't kids playing soldier. We were adults, preparing for combat. We were facing death and getting ready to kill other people. I had seen something in myself that I wasn't especially happy about. I'd always had moral and spiritual concerns – Gandhi, for instance, had been a hero of my youth – but there was plenty of aggression in me. I really had enjoyed firing that machine gun. But I hadn't enjoyed seeing men die, or realizing how much fear there was in the face of death. I gradually became convinced that I could serve only in a nonviolent way.

I approached our company commander, who was a West Point graduate and career soldier. He was a most impressive person, and I leveled with him. I told him that if I could just serve in the medical corps I would be an ideal soldier. He listened to what I had to say, questioning me closely. Finally he agreed and arranged for me to transfer. I finished my stint, and I believe I was a good soldier. But I'd had a deep realization of how precious life was and decided I didn't want to participate in the taking of it.

Not long after meeting Sivananda Saraswati I met another teacher who was to have a profound influence on my study of aging and death awareness, primarily because of one central experience. I have never identified this teacher in talks, referring to him as Badarayana, because he specifically requested that I not reveal his identity. He had no wish to be known or to teach a great many people. He had just four students when I knew him, but he felt that they were all potential teachers and that he would reach a larger audience through them.

I was still a university professor in those days, but I was trying to bring some of what I had learned from the Eastern tradition to my work. Badarayana attended a public talk I gave and came up afterward and offered himself as a teacher, saying he'd had a great deal of experience in both Hindu and Buddhist disciplines. I was suspicious at first, but he never asked for any payment, and his teaching seemed quite authentic. Again, it was mostly in the area of health and yoga, not so much in meditation.

We worked together for a number of years. At one point he suggested we go to a small Mexican coastal town where I had spent some time, Zihuatenejo, to do intensive work. We spent four months there, practicing yoga and studying.

One evening I was sitting in our cottage reading and Badarayana came in extremely excited, telling me that a major opportunity had come our way. Ten days earlier a Mexican laborer had gotten drunk and fallen into the bay. His body had not been recovered in all that time, but it had washed up on-shore that afternoon. His priest was coming from Mexico City for the body the next day, but for some religious reason that I never understood, the locals didn't want to sit with the corpse in the meantime. But they wanted someone to stay with it, and they thought of the two outsiders who were staying in town. They approached Badarayana, who was quite excited at the prospect.

I didn't understand his enthusiasm, and understood it even less when we got to the room. The corpse was in a large box packed with ice. The man seemed to have been big in the first place, but his corpse was also bloated, making him even bigger and distorting his features, and he was turning blue. There was a strong unpleasant odor. It was difficult even to enter the room. And we had agreed to be there all night.

Badarayana sat on one side of the box and I on the other. Soon he began teaching. "Not long ago this man was full of life. Now let's look at him." I, of course, felt a great deal of aversion, but Badarayana kept after me, insisting that I face this phenomenon and see what it brought up. There was fear. Nausea. Loathing. A strong wish to get out of the room. There was anger at Badarayana for putting me through all this.

We would be silent for periods of time, then he would check in with me, ask what I was really experiencing. That was the most valuable part of what we did. He also taught more directly. "This man was once alive. Now he is dead flesh. We too are subject to that lawfulness. What happens when you see that fact?"

I said that it was extremely painful. I didn't want to dwell on it.

"No, no," he said. "This man has a teaching for us. It's extremely valuable."

I wouldn't say that I entirely understood what Badarayana was getting at, but I gradually grew more comfortable sitting there and gained some sense of composure. I would still have been delighted to leave the room at any time.

Finally Badarayana said, "Why was I so enthusiastic about coming here?" I said that it was to show us how precious life is. "That's true," he said, "but you can also go deeper. This is a great incentive to practice. It shows us that we don't have much time. That we have no idea how much time we do have. This man didn't know he would die when he did. Life is precious not just because it is life but because it is an opportunity to practice. That is the ultimate gift this man gives us. He offers us a strong motivation for spiritual practice."

Yoga practice taught me more about how to help the body age gracefully than Buddhism did. Buddhism is more concerned with intimately experiencing the true nature of the body, seeing that it is insubstantial and not who we are. Although the Buddha was well aware of the health benefits of walking, moderation in diet, and healthy breathing, he didn't make those issues primary. One of my teachers in Thailand years later, Ajaan Buddhadasa, said that yogic understanding and practices could probably be taken for granted among meditators at the time of the Buddha. It was part of the spiritual culture of ancient India.

Buddhism goes deeply into the practice of death awareness. Cemetery contemplations, for instance, are included in the *Satipatthana Sutra,* which I think of as the declaration of independence for vipassana meditators. It boldly declares that deeply establishing awareness of the mind-body process can liberate us from suffering.

As I got involved in Buddhist practice, I began doing some meditations on my own death, with Thai, Sri Lankan, and Burmese monks. *Maranasati* – or death awareness – is a standard, highly respected, and highly valued practice in these countries, and meditators commonly practice it. It hasn't caught on much in this country because American teachers haven't emphasized it. But it clearly has real value, and I have gradually brought it into my teaching, for a variety of reasons.

For one thing, my students and I are not getting any younger. The subject has naturally become more a part of our consciousness. My father's death a few years ago also had a major impact on me. He had been a larger-than-life character, full of personality, and suddenly he was a corpse. Later he was some ashes in an urn, which I kept on my meditation shrine for some time, and now he is part of the Atlantic Ocean, where I scattered the ashes. The most important fact, of course, was that he had been my father. We'd been extremely close, and I loved him.

Krishnamurti's death also had a huge impact, because of my deep love and devotion to him and his clear, powerful teachings. He was a gentle, unassuming man in a personal context, but when he spoke he was on fire. It was as if God were speaking through him. Nevertheless, he too was subject to this inevitable law. All of his remarkable vitality was gone.

So I began to teach death awareness, but I have been careful about how I've introduced it to people. The first time I taught it, one of my students – a big, strapping man – literally bolted from the room in a panic attack. That made me even more cautious. Death awareness practice is definitely not for everyone and is not appropriate for just any time and place. It is a helpful teaching only when the student is ready for it, when it can intensify the commitment to dharma practice.

Sooner or later we all have to face the fact of death. We think of life and death as opposites, life as happening now and death as something that will happen at the end of the road, preferably an extremely long road. There is a certain unconscious arrogance that goes along with this attitude. Other people may be old; others may be ill, dying, or dead; but we are alive and well and (comparatively) young, and we'll deal with those problems when the time comes.

Our culture is particularly culpable in this regard. We put young people on pedestals, sick people in hospitals, elderly people in nursing homes; we sanitize the dead in funeral homes, trying to make them look attractive and alive, and do everything we can to keep death out of our consciousness. We put all of our energy into acquisition – of material possessions, knowledge, titles, land, friends, and lovers. We think we want these things for themselves, but we are using them to create and enhance our sense of self. This life of acquisition seems to shield us from the bedrock realities of aging and death. Our things become who we think we are.

Introduction

The truth is that we are aging from the moment we are born, that we have no idea when we may grow ill and when we will die. No one is guaranteed even one more breath. Death will take all our acquisitions away, including our sense of who we are, of everything we identify as self. Death is not waiting for us at the end of the road. It is walking with us the whole time. We are fascinated by disaster epics, like the story of the *Titanic*, but the truth is that we are all on the *Titanic*, right now. We just imagine it's a pleasure cruise, just as the people on the *Titanic* did.

At the same time, we harbor a huge amount of unfelt fear about sickness, aging, and death, and that fear robs us of vitality, partly because we expend so much energy avoiding and repressing it. Bringing up this fear and facing it – as I did with Badarayana and other teachers – is a great enhancement to our lives. Really facing death enables us to appreciate and make the best use of our life in a whole new way.

Finally, of course, Buddhist practice is about liberation, awakening, nirvana. It is about coming to the deathless. The attachments we form when we live, and that we will have to let go of when we die, are actually what make us suffer while we are here. The Buddha was quite clear on this subject: Clinging to things, especially to a sense of self, is what creates suffering. The knowledge that we have to let go of our attachments in death might enable us to let go of them now and save us a great deal of suffering. If we die to our attachments now, we won't need to later and won't feel so much fear of death when it comes. The shining light of death can liberate our life.

In addressing the practice of death awareness, the Buddha

left us five contemplations, which he advised us to reflect on frequently.

1. I am subject to aging. Aging is unavoidable.
2. I am subject to illness. Illness is unavoidable.
3. I am subject to death. Death is unavoidable.
4. I will grow different, separate from all that is dear and appealing to me.
5. I am the owner of my actions, heir to my actions, born of my actions, related through my actions, and live dependent on my actions. Whatever I do, for good or for ill, to that will I fall heir.

This isn't the cheeriest set of reflections in the world, and most people, when they first hear them, feel some resistance. They don't mind contemplating the Buddhist doctrine of impermanence in the world around them, but this is getting a little close to home. What is being asked of us as meditators is to come face-to-face with the law of impermanence in an intimate way.

These reflections have not been a major part of Buddhist practice in this country. In the sixties, when Buddhism first got popular here, people were coming to it out of the drug culture, looking for another way to get high. They weren't looking for anything as heavy as death awareness. They just wanted to feel better.

But in the Asian countries where Buddhism has been established for centuries, the practice of death awareness is an ancient and venerable tradition, and many meditators work with it. In fact, there are some who regard death awareness as the ultimate practice. The Buddha himself left behind such a statement. "Of all the footprints," he said, "that of the elephant is supreme. Similarly, of all mindfulness meditation, that on death is supreme."

Though these contemplations may sound morbid and depressing, working with them can have quite the opposite effect. Students often report – and I have experienced myself – a certain lightheartedness that comes from practicing them, a feeling of calm and ease. Many of us are carrying around a great deal of unacknowledged fear on the subject of death, and like any other fear, it weighs us down. Practicing death awareness helps flush out this fear, enabling us to face it and showing us that it too is an impermanent formation that is empty of self. The fear lingers in our consciousness when we don't acknowledge it and let it live out its life.

Death is a fact of existence, one that we all must face sometime. And death awareness is a real aid to practice. A deep understanding of mortality can often lead to awakening. Seeing that we don't have forever becomes a real motivating factor.

In Pali this phenomenon is known as *samvega:* the urgent need to practice that can grow out of a heightened sense of the perishable nature of life. It can include a real feeling of shock and a sense not only that life doesn't last forever but also that the way we have been living is wrong. It might turn our world upside down, sending us off to a whole new way of life. Even if it doesn't have so dramatic an effect, it can light a fire under our practice. We get much less caught up in power, prestige, money, lust, the acquisition of goods. Dharma teachings start to make real sense to us, and we begin to live them instead of just assenting intellectually. *Samvega* leads to a conversion of the heart, from an egocentric existence to a search for that which is timeless, vast, and sacred.

An important accompaniment to *samvega* is the Pali concept of *pasada,* which might be translated as clear and serene confidence, a conviction that our situation isn't hopeless, that the practice of meditation can take us beyond sickness, aging, and death. The problem surrounding these phenomena is not external to us. It has everything to do with our cravings and attachments. Suffering is not a dead end but a gateway to realization. The proper application of the practice – of the eightfold path – can turn the pain of sickness and death into the joy of liberation.

It would be cruel just to open people up to the realization of their transience without giving them a way out. Buddhist teaching offers us a way to move beyond impermanence to the deathless.

Many readers will be familiar with the legendary story of the Buddha's life. It was predicted at his birth that he would be either a sage or a ruler, and his father – who himself was a chief and wanted his son to follow in his footsteps – kept him confined to the palace and saw to it that his every wish was gratified. The young man married at the age of sixteen and had a family, but when he was twenty-five a vague yearning made him break away from the palace grounds to discover the outside world.

Out in the world he encountered three kinds of people he had never seen before: an old man, bent with age; another who was extremely sick; and a man who was dead and being carried to the charnel grounds. He was shocked by these sights, shaken to the core of his being. And on the way back to the palace he saw a wandering contemplative who seemed to have found a deep peace, and he resolved to live as that man did.

Thus did the Buddha first encounter the three phenomena that are the subject of our study. He also found the answer to them, the way out of the whole dilemma.

Our five contemplations dovetail rather nicely with the messengers the Buddha encountered. The fourth contemplation – I will grow different, separate from all that is dear to me – reflects what the wandering contemplative had chosen to do before death forced him to. He effected these separations at the time so he would not suffer from them later.

The monk who leaves home renounces sex, family, wealth, and most possessions, giving up all forms of luxury as a strategy to optimize the possibility for true liberation. He is trying to enhance the potential that we all have to free ourselves from suffering. But monasticism and lay practice are both conventions; neither is absolute truth.

In the deepest and most profound sense, the fourth messenger is symbolic of inner freedom, which is available to all human beings. Our task is the same as his, to abandon our craving and our clinging. Krishnamurti conveyed that message constantly. We must die every day. We must die every moment. We must die now.

The fifth contemplation is the one that doesn't have a parallel in the messengers. It refers to the law of karma, the doctrine of rebirth, and certainly, in a book on the subject of death, I will deal with it. But it is also a place where people get lost, wrapped up in abstract speculation about what their past lives were, what their future lives might be, all of which can turn into a mind game. It can be yet another way to avoid practice. I believe the law of karma is absolutely true – our actions do have consequences, in this life if not in future ones – but I am not particularly interested in speculating on it. I try to stay with the present moment.

Our task is to free ourselves from karma, not in the sense of avoiding it but by getting to a place where it doesn't matter. The fifth is an important contemplation, in some ways the most important, because it offers an answer to the bleak news of the other four. Our final focus is the fourth messenger, the one who is practicing in order to free himself, and the fourth contemplation, our need to die to our attachments now. That is the best karma.

It is natural for people to concern themselves with the profound and important question of whether there is life after death. But this book focuses on this question: Is there life before death? We are looking for the light that death can shed on life.

With that in mind, we turn to our first contemplation.

Note: At the heart of my teaching about aging and death – and about everything else – is awareness practice, which includes, specifically, the vital practice of sitting meditation. It may be difficult to follow the teachings in this book if you don't have some knowledge of that practice, so I have written

Introduction

a brief overview of it as an appendix. Anyone not familiar with awareness practice should turn to the appendix before proceeding to the first chapter.[1]

---

1. I cover the same ground in much more detail in my book *Breath by Breath: The Liberating Practice of Insight Meditation* (Boston: Shambhala Publications, 1998).

THE FIRST MESSENGER
Aging Is Unavoidable

"Not wanting things to change." If we think like this, we must suffer. When we think that the body is ourselves or belongs to us, we are afraid when we see it change.

– AJAAN CHAH

I am subject to aging. Aging is unavoidable.

JUST TO SPEND some time with this contemplation every day would be instructive, to see it and really penetrate it. People often get impatient when you tell them something like that. I *know* I'm aging, they say. And we do know it, intellectually, in the abstract. Then again we don't. We don't know it in our hearts. We don't know it in our bones. And we don't live it. The slightest sign of aging comes up and we do everything we can to avoid it.

I'm not talking just about face-lifts, hair dye, hairpieces, adopting the fashions of young people. (And I'm not necessarily opposed to such things.) I am talking about being aware of what your body is going through. I'm talking about knowing that you – like everyone and everything else – are subject to the law of impermanence, and that that law includes not just eventual death but gradual changes along the way. I'm talking about forgetting the image you project, and knowing what is happening to you.

I'm also talking about experiences that happen to perfectly ordinary people, all the time. One happened to me not long ago that really knocked some wisdom into me and has given my students many a laugh as I have recounted it. I am a person who takes very good care of himself. I do yoga most mornings; I take long vigorous walks; I meditate a great deal; and I am careful about food supplements and the food that I eat.

About three years ago, when I was sixty-three, I was on the subway in Boston, coming back from a trip to the dentist. I comfort myself with the thought that I may have looked a little peaked from my dental work. I was standing there holding on to the metal rail when a young woman seated in front of me smiled and stood up and gave me her seat. I didn't realize at first quite what was happening. I thought she was getting off at the next stop. But that stop went by, and the next, and I started to realize: Wait a minute. A young woman just gave me her seat on the subway.

My mind started racing. I wanted to say to her: You've got it all wrong. I get up and give my seat to you. I've been giving up subway seats all my life. But apparently, from her standpoint, this looked appropriate. She was a young, vigorous, healthy woman. And I, it seems, looked like a man who needed to sit down. All my years of doing yoga, eating good food, and taking long walks were wasted. I looked my age anyway. Next time it would be, "Hey, Grandpa. How'd you like a seat?" Or,

Aging Is Unavoidable

"Slow down, old-timer. Let me help you with those packages." My self-image as a youthful, bouncy "older man" – an image I didn't even know I had – had been smashed to pieces.

This was not a bad experience. It was actually good. A young woman made a courteous gesture, and I got to take a load off my feet. It was what I did with it – before my awareness returned and I had a good laugh at myself – that mattered. It was a modern-day rite of passage, an initiatory moment that let me know I was in a new category. It shattered my self-image.

Self-images are a problem. They are designed to help us feel adequate and secure but also often cause a great deal of suffering. We all have them, and most of us aren't aware we do. We spend enormous time and energy and even money creating and protecting them, trying to keep them intact while our daily experience is chipping away at them. Then when someone sees us in a different way, we are shattered. They mention a senior-citizen discount, and suddenly we see ourselves in Bermuda shorts and canvas shoes, wearing a funny little straw hat. That isn't the image we want to present at all. The pictures we have in our own head are way out of date.

What we normally do is create a new image: Yes, I may strictly speaking be eligible for the senior-citizen discount, but I don't look it (unless I've just been to the dentist). I'm quite spry for my age. I have the strength of a man twenty years younger. You can keep your seat on the subway (though I will take the lower fare).

I am not, I repeat, opposed to looking after one's health and appearance. I believe in taking care of the body, and that includes dressing well and being clean and well groomed. Doing so is just a matter of expressing one's human dignity and doesn't mean we are self-centered.

But the practice is about moving beyond all images, being intimate with the raw, naked experience of your body, its moment-by-moment experience. The Buddha spoke in several of his sutras of the body within the body. What he meant was the body as it really is. Not the image we have of it but the body as it is right now, the sensations evident to us as we sit reading this book.

The great baseball pitcher Satchel Paige had a much more down-to-earth way of putting it, but he was saying the same thing. When he was in his prime as a pitcher, African-American players were confined to what were then called the Negro leagues, and by the time he finally got to the majors he was quite old for a ballplayer. Reporters naturally asked him about his age, and he said, "Age isn't a problem. It's a question of mind over matter. If you don't mind, it doesn't matter."

How Mind-States Happen

Let's have a look at a concrete example, one that is less whimsical. At the Cambridge Insight Meditation Center, where I teach, I regularly give interviews at which students can come in and talk to me about their formal sitting practice or their daily lives. On one recent morning, a student told me she'd been experiencing a great deal of sadness and fear about aging. I asked her to be more specific, and she said that that morning she had awakened with some stiffness in her back and knees. Perhaps she pictured a grandmother or some other elderly relative who was stiff in the morning, and suddenly this relatively young woman – she was just in her mid-forties – thought, "This is it. Old age is here."

Within seconds she was picturing a really stiff body, one that could never straighten out; white hair, wrinkled skin, the loss of all attractiveness; a cane, then a walker, finally a wheelchair; she saw her body deteriorating, her mind starting to go, her final years full of illness and pain. Furthermore, she hadn't put enough away for retirement, so she imagined destitution as well, an old woman who needed special care but couldn't afford it. She saw herself on the street, wrapped in a ragged overcoat and shivering, asking passersby for money.

In reality, she was an attractive professional woman in her forties, living in a perfectly comfortable house. But as far as her suffering went, she might as well have been out on the street already. Such is the power of the mind. It can take a simple unpleasant sensation and turn it into a powerful sense of self.

We have all experienced such flights of fancy, sudden feelings of terror. And I would be the first to admit that they conceal a certain wisdom. Old age, sickness, and death are the fate of most of us – death, for all of us – so in that way she was seeing something real. Furthermore, the need to provide for your old age is a real one that needs to be attended to. Sometimes you experience exaggerated anxiety because there is some real task that you need to do.

At the same time, this was an almost classic case of a

process that the Buddha talked about quite eloquently, the way that the mind turns physical sensations into suffering. It is an excellent example for us to work with. So I would like to spend some time on it.

Of the various phenomena that can arise in the body and mind, one that the Buddha spoke about specifically is designated by the Pali word *vedana,* which is often translated as "feelings." *Vedana* doesn't actually refer to what we think of in our culture as feelings but just to sensations, anything that might come through the six sense doors (in Buddhism, the mind is considered a sense).

The Buddha said there are three kinds of *vedana,* to which we have three characteristic reactions. A sensation might be pleasant, in which case we tend to hold on to it or want to repeat it. It might be unpleasant, so we are inclined to push it away. And it might be neutral. In the case of neutral sensations, we tend to get bored or fill in the emptiness with fantasy. Either way, we're not present with the sensation.

For my student, the feeling was unpleasant but just mildly so; a little morning stiffness is not exactly a heart attack. But the act of pushing it away was quite elaborate. It also traded a minor physical discomfort for a severe mental one. It took a mild physical pain and turned it into torment.

Another phenomenon that might turn up as we watch the body and mind is what the Buddha called mind-states. These are more complicated than sensations; they typically combine a racing mind, piling-up thoughts (like the ones about aging that we've just seen), with noticeable sensations in the body. There are various mind-states, but three that the Buddha emphasized repeatedly in his teachings he called the *kilesas,* or three mental poisons. They are greed, hatred, and delusion, sometimes rendered as passion, aversion, and confusion.

Greed is the feeling of wanting something we don't have. Hatred is the feeling of wanting something to be gone that we do have. And delusion is when we don't know what we want or don't see clearly what is present. There is a fog over the mind.

The *kilesas* in general are rooted in delusion, or ignorance. Ignorance is the real basis of all our craving and aversion. So you could say that the source of my student's problem was delusion, concretely manifesting itself as aversion. Something was present that she didn't want to be there. She began to struggle with it. And her mind-states proliferated.

The Buddha was once asked how such a situation differed for someone who is enlightened, as opposed to someone who isn't. And he said the unenlightened person is like a warrior who is hit with two arrows. In my student's case, the first arrow was the stiffness. The second was the emotional turmoil that she made out of it. The first arrow is unavoidable. There are pains and difficulties that are simply a part of being human (and many of them are linked with our larger subjects, aging, sickness, and death). The Buddha never claimed we could avoid them.

But we can avoid the second arrow. We don't need to take physical suffering and make it into torment. We can feel the stiffness and let it be stiffness. What's the problem? It is an impermanent phenomenon like any other.

So a person with some degree of awakening would feel the

stiffness. She might feel it as unpleasant. But it would end right there.

That's easy to say, of course. That kind of liberation is the result of long hard practice (though it is also available right now. In this moment you can feel a sensation and let it be what it is. You don't need to turn it into torment. Early in the practice, this includes some willfulness. An awakened person no longer has to will it). In the case of the woman who came to the interview, she found herself rapidly transported – in a matter of seconds – into the complex mind-state known as fear. There were probably unpleasant feelings in the body and thoughts piling up one after another. If she was like most of us, the thoughts were more vivid. At the time, they seemed to represent reality. She was going to wind up destitute and die a long, slow, painful death full of suffering.

There are several ways to work with such a mind-state. In the interview, we fell back on reflection. We looked at the thoughts that arose and saw which were totally fanciful and which had some basis in reality. But our encounter was taking place after the mind-state had largely passed. At the actual moment when it was happening, she was quite overwhelmed by fear, and probably the best tactic would have been to bring her attention to the breathing. That wouldn't have been repression; she would have been acknowledging her fear but acknowledging also that it was too much for her, that she needed to give her attention to something else for a while, to calm down and then perhaps be able to examine fear directly.

But once her mindfulness had developed to a greater extent, she could work with her fear in an even more valuable way. She could observe it just as it is, without adding to or subtracting from it in any way. She would see it arise out of the uncomfortable sensation of stiffness, see it proliferate as feelings in the body and thoughts in the mind, and see it eventually pass away, like any other phenomenon. She would see that fear itself is impermanent; though it seems to be solid and overwhelming when it is present, it actually lacks any essential core and is empty of self. Once she had deeply seen that, fear would be much less of a problem for her.

We can learn to turn our attention to the energy we call fear and sustain that state of observation. With practice our reflexes grow quicker and the practice becomes easier; we remember to observe rather than to avoid. We needn't be held captive by a lifetime of unexamined fear. Our situation isn't hopeless.

One way to work with aging is to take up such a contemplation intentionally, to take some time every day to reflect on the fact: I am subject to aging. Aging is unavoidable. We might allow the significance of these thoughts to sink in, or imagine what it would be like to be old and infirm, to move slowly, to have limited physical powers, to be dependent on others. Many people are in this state right now, and we see them with a blind arrogance, the arrogance of (comparative) youth and health. But we are all subject to the same law. We are brothers and sisters in our liability to sickness, aging, and death.

Whatever feelings come up around this contemplation, you work with them as I've suggested, let them be and just observe them. Over time you will flush out a great deal of previously unfelt fear.

Another way to work with aging might be called naturalistic observation, using the kinds of examples I've brought up, the small things that happen every day in our lives. Often we suppress these things and try not to notice them, or at the other extreme grow depressed and panicky, lost in our identification with the aging condition of the body. But in practicing with these incidents, and with the mind-states that arise, we do something very valuable. We liberate ourselves from the mind-states and from aging itself. That doesn't mean we don't age. It means that the mind doesn't suffer from the body's aging.

We have emphasized in this discussion the tendency of the mind to attach to the physical signs of aging and make self out of them. Our youthful images are shattered and unflattering pictures of being old break in and bring us sorrow and even torment. But it isn't just a matter of image-making. Real changes take place. We can't run or think as fast. We have less strength and stamina. Our coordination, memory, and sexual powers may diminish. We may lose our job or be viewed in a marginal way after having been a central player.

Such losses are not just a matter of self-image. And though we might need to mourn them, it doesn't follow that our loss of capacity needs to be a source of torment. The reflections that we've discussed can help us face our losses and come to terms gracefully with the way things are.

One of the most vivid experiences of impermanence that I ever had took place when I was working on my Ph.D. in social psychology at the University of Chicago. I was old-fashioned even in those days and saw myself as a student of human behavior; a notebook and ballpoint pen were sophisticated-enough tools for me. But I worked in a department that insisted on an extremely scientific – meaning technological – brand of research, and they had me working on a computer, one of the first that came out. It used FORTRAN; it took up a whole room, made a huge amount of noise, and spit out reams of paper.

I didn't want to work with such a monstrosity, but the chairperson of my thesis committee insisted, so I had to relate to this massive computer and the people operating it. I would take them my data and didn't really understand what they were doing with it. They had a complex technological language, which only they knew, and I had my work, which they didn't know or care about. Sometimes I would show up quite excited about what I'd found, and they would say, "Don't bother us with the content. Just give us the data. Give us the variables."

One day I walked in, and it looked as if they were staging a funeral. The whole team was there, more people than were usually around. Everyone seemed incredibly depressed. I said, "What's all the gloom and doom?" And they said, "A new program has been invented. It's drastically simpler and faster, and all of a sudden we're obsolete. We've spent ten years learning this, and we're a museum piece. In the meantime, there are all these young people who are familiar with the new system. They're taking off, and we're left behind."

It really struck me: Don't tie your life to anything subject to time, because sooner or later it will fail you. That goes for the latest computer system. It also goes for our life in human form. As the Buddha told us, we do not find ultimate fulfillment there.

RIGHTING THE BALANCE

There are other forms of practice that deal – somewhat indirectly – with the aging process. One of them is called *asubha* meditation, meditation on the unloveliness of the body. It revolves around a classification system in which the body is divided into thirty-two parts. You learn the parts as they are traditionally listed, take them up one by one, recite them inwardly, and reflect on them. You begin with the hair on the head, go on to the skin, the fingernails, the teeth, and so on.

After a while you start to unzip the body and look at what is inside. You find blood, urine, feces, all kinds of unsavory substances. If you've developed any kind of *samadhi* – a concentrated, peaceful, collected state of mind – before you begin, the practice becomes quite vivid. It once made me nauseous. It also wipes out any chance for feeling sexual attraction, and is thus used to help celibate monks diminish sexual feeling. It can also be of immense help in seeing the true nature of the body: there is this body, but it isn't me or mine.

The first time I was exposed to *asubha* meditation, I was doing a retreat at the Insight Meditation Society. The Burmese teacher U Sulananda started to describe this practice during a dharma talk. I had been doing hatha yoga, valuing mindful breathing and good food, keeping myself in shape. I had a somewhat romantic view of things. All of a sudden this teacher started to talk about the foulness of the body. You could see people realize: This guy's really going into all this. They were immediately uncomfortable. Some actually left. I thought: This couldn't be what the Buddha had in mind. He was interested in enlightenment and awakening, the beauty of life. In those days, if a practice didn't fit our model of what was aesthetically or ethically agreeable, we just threw it out. No more *asubha* meditation for us.

Ten years later I took up this practice for an intense six-week period with Ajaan Suwat of Thailand. I told him about the aversion and doubt that had cut short my first experience. He laughed heartily and let me know that the point of *asubha* meditation wasn't just to bring up aversion. It was to counteract our tremendous identification with and attachment to the body, our infatuation with it. With some practice you can get very good at running through the parts of the body. If you're drawn to a particular part, you can work with that a great deal. I, for instance, felt an affinity for the skeleton. I'd been intrigued with skeletons ever since I was a child. So I worked with that.

After I did this practice for a few weeks, my mind became very concentrated and I started seeing everyone as skeletons, seeing myself as one too. At other times internal bodily organs like the blood, stomach, and intestines appeared quite vividly to me. Once I even got nauseous when it came time to eat, because I pictured the food on its journey. When I really got skillful, the teacher changed the instructions. I had completely deconstructed the body, and now he said, "Now put it back together. Make it pretty again." Because that is also true. The body is a miracle. So I would do that, and then he'd have me deconstruct it again. I got very good at going back and forth.

The point is to develop a middle way. Not to worship the body, becoming attached to it; and also not to reject it, ignoring it altogether. That spiritual tradition exists also, total rejection of the body, seeing it as something that is in the way and that we need to overcome. The Buddha studied in that ascetic tradition for a while, but he eventually rejected it quite pointedly. He practiced moderation in taking care of the body in order to make proper use of it. But he also didn't get attached to it, because it is constantly changing and eventually gives out altogether.

So we're moving toward a balanced view. There is this body. No one denies it exists. It just doesn't have the existence we think it does. It is an impermanent changing phenomenon. Above all, we don't identify it as me or mine. At first when we say that, it is an ideology. But if we meditate long enough, we see it as a reality. The body is definitely here. (It also definitely ages.) But no one owns it.

We can also read the section on aging in the *Dhammapada*,[1] an ancient crystallization of the Buddha's teaching into verse form, in the light of what we've said about *asubha* meditation. The first stanza makes reference to some women followers of the Buddha who were frivolous and lighthearted

---

1. Thanissaro Bhikkhu, *"Dhammapada," a Translation* (Barre, Mass.: Barre Center for Buddhist Studies, Dhamma Dana Publications, 1998).

and would come to his talks in a festive mood after they had been drinking. He is speaking directly to them.

> What laughter, why joy,
> when constantly aflame?
> Enveloped in darkness,
> don't you look for a lamp?

The flame referred to in the second line is that of desire, of craving, the same flame the Buddha spoke of in his famous fire sermon, where he declared that the whole world is on fire with greed, hatred, and delusion. The women are festive but don't see how enslaved they are to their craving. The darkness that envelops them is that of ignorance. They should be looking for a light.

The second stanza makes reference to a renowned courtesan who had recently died. It seems to see her simultaneously at various moments in her life, so that even her beautiful image – apparently enhanced by cosmetics – is concealing a grim future.

> Look at the beautified image,
> a heap of festering wounds, shored up:
> ill, but the object of many resolves,
> where there is nothing lasting or sure.

The "many resolves" that the body is the "object" of are the desires of many men to sleep with her. This stanza seems to refer to the two views of the body we've mentioned, the beautified self-image and the body within the body, which is decaying all the time. It's as if the stanza says: If you could see what this body will eventually become, you would not be so attached to it.

The third stanza continues the same kind of imagery. It resembles *asubha* meditation itself, arousing fear and aversion as a corrective to the idealization of the body.

> Worn out is this body,
> a nest of diseases, dissolving.
> This putrid conglomeration
> is bound to break up,
> for life is hemmed in with death.

The fourth refers to another kind of Buddhist meditation. Monks would visit the charnel grounds to contemplate bodies in various states of decomposition. They would contemplate skeletons, then the isolated bones that were left when the skeletons broke up. Over time the bones would decompose into dust, and the monks would contemplate that. Then the dust would blow away, and literally nothing would be left of what had once been a human being.

> On seeing these bones
> discarded
> like gourds in the fall,
> pigeon-gray:
> what delight?

The story behind this stanza is that there was a group of young monks who believed they had achieved enlightenment, when really they had just attained a degree of concentration. The Buddha took them to the charnel grounds, to see what equanimity they could exhibit there. They realized they needed to continue practicing.

The fifth stanza makes reference to a beautiful queen who had little interest in the Buddha's teaching but was much enamored of her own form. The Buddha showed her an image of it, then caused it to age as she watched, just showing her a more rapid version of the inevitable change that was already happening.

> A city made of bones,
> plastered over with flesh & blood,
> whose hidden treasures are:
> pride & contempt
> aging & death.

The sixth stanza lets us know that this law of impermanence is no respecter of wealth, that royal families are just as subject to it as anyone else. It also refers to a part of us that doesn't age.

> Even royal chariots
> well-embellished
> get run down,
> and so does the body
> succumb to old age.
> But the Dhamma of the good
> doesn't succumb to old age:
> the good let the civilized know.

The "good" are the people in touch with this deep truth; the "civilized" are those readily available to be trained, people like ourselves directly penetrating aging on their way to that which is timeless.

The seventh stanza points to the situation of people without inner development, describing someone who matures physically but not spiritually.

> This unlistening man
> matures like an ox.
> His muscles develop,
> his discernment not.

The eighth and ninth are two of the most famous in the *Dhammapada* and are known as the "Song of Victory."

> Through the round of many births I roamed
> without reward,
> without rest,
> seeking the house-builder.
> Painful is birth
> again & again.

> House-builder, you're seen!
> You will not build a house again.
> All your rafters broken,
> the ridge pole destroyed,
> gone to the Unformed, the mind
> has come to the end of craving.

At first glance these stanzas seem to be a departure from the subject of aging and to take up death and rebirth. We in the West don't take rebirth for granted, and some don't believe in it at all. Here the speaker has achieved nirvana and will no longer be subject to the round of death and rebirth. Seen in another way, however, these stanzas are about the here and now. In this life the self is reborn every time we attach to something as being me or mine, to a mood, a sensation, a mind-state. This series of rebirths is quite literally exhausting; it is a full-time job to attend to the ego with its many desires and aversions, its various wounds.

This is the kind of rebirth that takes place when we feel stiffness and think, "I am an old person"; suddenly we are reborn in a new form, to a whole new world of suffering. Once we clearly see this process at work, we have the option of not participating in it. Then the "I" is not created; the house is not built. We can discover nirvana in the midst of everyday life.

The last two stanzas refer to people who are not able to choose between the life of the spirit and the life of the world. Just as it is possible to live in both at once, it is possible to live in neither, by not fully entering into life. Your days become stale and flat.

> Neither living the chaste life
> nor gaining wealth in their youth,
> they waste away like old herons
> in a dried-up lake
> depleted of fish.

> Neither living the chaste life
> nor gaining wealth in their youth,
> they lie around,
> misfired from the bow,
> sighing over old times.

Whose Mind Do We Lose?

The "Song of Victory" makes reference to the Unborn, also known by many other names: the unconditioned, the deathless, buddha nature, nirvana, our true nature. Strictly speaking, this subject comes up later in the five contemplations of *maranasati;* it is more concerned with death itself.

But as I've just suggested, it also permeates everything we're discussing, all of Buddhist teaching, because it doesn't refer to a state in the future or in the past. It refers to a state we're living in right now. The *Heart Sutra,* a Mahayana teaching, tells us that form is emptiness, which we've already seen; all phenomena are impermanent and insubstantial. But it also says that emptiness is form. The empty state that we believe ourselves to be seeking is right here in the world of form. We should not look for it elsewhere.

I bring this up now because, in all of the classes and practice groups that I teach on the subject of aging and death, one kind of question comes up again and again. Though many of my students are middle-aged and beyond, I have students of all ages, and they tend to be addressing issues of aging and death. It might not be that they themselves are ill or near dying but that a parent or relative is. They come to the classes with their fears and concerns. We are trying not to sweep these matters under the rug anymore. We are facing them as part of our lives and our practice.

And though people do raise questions about physical illness and about death itself, the question that seems to come up most often is about aging, and a certain aspect of the mind.

Aging Is Unavoidable

Students can understand how the practice will help them if they are facing a physical illness like cancer. They understand how – if we can stay alert – the practice will be a great help at the moment of death. But what, they want to know, if we become senile? What if our brain starts to go? What if the condition we're dealing with undermines our ability to practice at all?

We fear cancer; we fear AIDS and a number of other diseases. We fear the possibility that we will be reduced to a state of helpless dependency. But more than anything else, it seems, we fear Alzheimer's disease and other diseases of the brain. We fear that as we approach death we will not be in full possession of our mental faculties. What then?

I don't know, obviously. Ask me after I've lost my mind. It is like what one of my favorite Korean monks, Byok Jo Sunim, who absolutely radiated energy and joy, once said to me. He seemed to me a highly awakened person, so I asked him what happened after we died. "I don't know," he said. "I haven't died yet." In all the teachings on aging and death, there are some that seem speculative and others that are based on experience. I would like to stay as close as possible to concrete experience.

I have had some experiences that shed light on this matter. There was a great Indian teacher, for instance, Sri Nisargadatta Maharaj, who taught to a very old age, and when he was in his eighties someone asked him what it was like to be an old yogi. And he said, "Oh, I just watch senility come in. I see the memory decompose on an almost daily basis." And he roared with laughter.

Perhaps he is suggesting that there is something larger and deeper than the thinking mind, or the brain, something that can observe it all.

Many of us have had intimations of that larger mind. If you've ever had the experience of observing your thinking, you've realized that awareness is larger than the thinker. The further you get into meditation, the more you become this observer. It's as if you crawl out on a limb, observing more and more of who you are, until finally you saw the limb off. You are observation itself. Pure awareness. And that awareness is not itself affected by anything. It just is. Everything else is scenery.

Ajaan Chah, a revered and much-loved Thai forest master, had an unsuccessful operation that left him with something like water on the brain at the end of his life. I'm not really sure what his exact condition was, but for the last four or five years of his life he was unable to communicate.

We need to be careful, of course, about idolizing the teacher; there are often stories about the end of a teacher's life that may be largely romantic projection. But people say that even though Ajaan Chah couldn't talk, he was wonderful to be around. His very presence was a teaching. Which is to say that, though he couldn't talk, he was still present and clearly at peace. Many people said their visits to him were uplifting, not depressing at all.

In the Thai forest tradition, this awakened part of us is called *buddho,* which might be roughly translated as "that which knows" (this word is sometimes used in meditation practice as a silent object of concentration, coordinating the first syllable with the in-breath, the second with the out-breath, repeating it over and over like a mantra). We all are this absolute presence, but we haven't fully tapped into it; we do that as we meditate, and the more we practice the deeper we get. We learn to recognize awareness itself, and how to live and act from such silent clarity.

But the time to start practicing is now. You don't want to wait until you've had a stroke or are in the early stages of Alzheimer's. The more you've entered that state of deep awareness, the more available it is to you. In these situations we fear, where our mind has been affected, that place will be our refuge. As Suzuki Roshi said, "One purpose of our practice is to enjoy our old age. But we can't fool ourselves. Only sincere practice will work."

I have a friend who is in the early stages of Alzheimer's. He has been diagnosed and knows he has Alzheimer's, but he has also been practicing insight meditation for many years. He is definitely losing his memory, and I don't want to minimize that; when an instance of memory loss occurs, he can experience anything from disappointment to real terror. Sometimes he doesn't know who he is speaking to or why he is speaking. But he is able to see the terror.

At first his loss of memory in social situations was a nightmare. But his courage, help from his wife, and years of practicing meditation enabled him to remember to be mindful of his disorientation and his fears. He told me that when he awakens each morning, he has no idea of where he is or what he is supposed to do. He has learned to be mindful of such confusion and disorientation. He no longer panics. It passes, and he is able to get washed and ready for the day. So the episodes of memory loss became more and more manageable. He is now able to work with them as impermanent phenomena that come and go. He has the very real difficulty and sorrow of losing his memory, but it is no longer overwhelming.

I think the key question is: Can you live the life you have? Can you work with what you've got? One of my students used to care for the elderly, and she had some wonderful stories. One of her patients was ninety-three years old, was confined to a wheelchair, and had degenerative vision problems. My student took her Aldous Huxley's book *The Art of Seeing,* and when she came in to see her patient later the woman was doing the exercises in the book. She always had a sense of possibility; she would say, "I'm going to stand up and walk down this hallway," even though it wouldn't particularly change her condition; she just wanted to do it. She wanted to do what she could.

My colleague Christopher Titmuss, a fellow teacher at the Insight Meditation Society, told me an even more poignant story. He had a doctor friend at a hospital who wanted him to meet a particular patient, a woman who had had polio as a child and had been put in an iron lung. She had been confined that way for more than forty years. But when Christopher met her, she was smiling, just beaming. All the doctors and nurses loved to be around her; she was often happy and serene. Finally he asked, "How can you be so happy?" and she said, "Every now and then someone opens the window, and a breeze comes in."

So we work with what we have. We take what joy we can. We

have all perceived a breeze like that. How many of us have taken joy in it?

Finally, I would like to talk about my father, because he is the example I know best. He had Alzheimer's for several years before he died. And he, alas, was not a meditator. Every ounce of energy in his body, for most of his lifetime, was dedicated precisely to *not* being religious. He was a devoted ex-Marxist who continued to think that religion was the opiate of the masses. Being opposed to religion was his religion. He hated rabbis, priests, nuns. He thought they were all parasites. He was the rebellious child of fourteen generations of rabbis, so he had plenty of history with this subject.

In spite of my father's views, I had seven years of orthodox Jewish training as a child. He would take me aside and whisper, "Do it for your mother and your grandparents, but it's all a lot of nonsense." This was my father talking, and I believed him. Then much later, when I had discovered meditation and left my position at the university, he was horrified. I would visit my parents at their house, and of course would do my daily sitting meditation.

"It's like davening," he said, using the Jewish word for prayer. "You've reinstituted the lineage of rabbis! With all your education, you've gone back to this. How could you be so stupid? You're just like those old Jews. Why don't they do something useful with their lives?"

When he had Alzheimer's he would go in and out of clear mind-states. Sometimes he would seem intelligent, alert, and rational, then suddenly he'd be confused, *very* confused. He would mix up something in the present with something from eighty years before. There was a logic to it, but his wires were all crossed.

We had to put him in a nursing home because my mother couldn't handle him anymore, and when he first got there he hated it. He especially hated the food. On four different occasions he tried to escape. This was a man who couldn't walk, but he would somehow manage in his wheelchair to get past everyone and out the door. He would get up and fall in the snow, and someone would find him later. And when we visited him and had to leave, he would be terribly disappointed, as if we were abandoning him forever. That was extremely difficult for me. But at the same time, I could tell he knew that his mind wasn't right, that his reactions were too extreme. I could see it in his eyes.

After about two and a half years, things started to change. He started not to complain so much. He actually began to like the food. "Would you care to join me?" he'd say, as if it were a four-star restaurant.

Sometimes he seemed to be in such a state of peace that it was startling. I didn't know if I could trust it. He seemed more at peace than I was. One time, I remember, I came to the rest home and was fussing all over him. I'd brought him his favorite food – a bagel with cream cheese and lox – and I kept rubbing his back and saying how much I loved him. He looked at me with deep calm and said, "You don't have to try so hard. I love you, and I know you love me. It's okay."

Another time my wife said to him, "Dad, you've always been so pro-life, so full of vitality and vigor. You're a lover of life, and that's great." He sat quietly for several minutes, then said, "That's not true. I just learned the value of life six months ago." That really bowled us over. He had learned the value of life while he had Alzheimer's and spent his days in a wheelchair. He had continued to learn even when he was old and ill.

One time toward the end of his life, a number of us from the family came to visit him, and as we approached his room we heard him speaking in Russian. He had left Russia when he was fourteen, and he was now ninety. But he was speaking in Russian, very respectfully, to God. "Look. I know I haven't believed in you all these years. I really think it's all a lot of nonsense. But I'm coming to the end now, and I'm open. I really am. I'm open. But *show* me something. *Show* me. I don't see shit."

That only confirms my hunch that there's hope for all of us. Whatever shape we're in, there is a deep part of us that is still aware. It is the part that is open and wants to see something. Our practice is to begin to tap into it now.

THE SECOND MESSENGER
Illness Is Unavoidable

Though my body is sick, my mind shall not be sick. Thus,
householder, must you train yourself.

— THE BUDDHA *(Nakulapita Sutta)*

I am subject to illness. Illness is unavoidable.

THE DHARMA attitude toward illness, especially in the
Theravada tradition, is quite radical and very much in
contrast to the attitude of our culture. It isn't that the monks
in Asia want to get sick; they appreciate good health and the
energy that it gives for practice. But when the body does grow
ill, that too is considered a wonderful occasion for practice.

Illness, for one thing, is an immediate reminder of the un-
predictability of everything. It is a striking demonstration
of impermanence, a reminder that the body is a changing
phenomenon and does break down, sometimes quite rapidly.
Illness is also a reminder – one that we often ignore – that
the body will eventually give out altogether. Since that fact is
considered a vital part of practice, we make good use of the
reminder, the chance to see deeply into ourselves. We often

see what we are by seeing what we are not. And we are not permanent physical entities.

So as dharma practitioners we do whatever we reasonably can to be healed but don't bemoan the fact that we are ill and don't constantly compare our condition to a time when we were healthy. Illness provides a unique opportunity for practice, especially if we are bedridden. Suddenly we can drop all the responsibilities and cares of daily life.

It is like a mini-retreat, except that we're flat on our backs. We have an opportunity to observe our bodily sensations and our mind in a minute fashion. The sensations themselves are often quite vivid when we are ill. They might involve pain, which provides us with a wonderful opportunity to strengthen our practice.

This attitude is much in contrast to that of our culture (and probably – to be fair – to that of most cultures). We are an energetic, productive, can-do society, proud of our robust health, and we see disease as something that shouldn't be happening, when it is really just a natural part of being human, of finding ourselves in a body that is changing and not entirely under our control.

Just watch advertisements for cold remedies on television. All of them involve getting people on their feet and back to the office as soon as possible. The cold medicine that best disguises the symptoms is presented as the one to buy.

It is natural to want to feel well. But these advertisements make it look as if productive work is the only important thing in life. Ancient cultures understood that there are other important things as well.

The well-known vipassana teacher S. N. Goenka is a case in point. He started off as a businessman in Burma and was quite successful. The only problem was that he had acute migraine headaches, which were probably related to the stress he was under. He consulted doctors all over Asia, Europe, and the United States. The only relief he found was from doses of morphine, but doctors told him that if he continued with that he would eventually be addicted. So he sought other means.

A friend suggested he try vipassana meditation, on a ten-day retreat led by Sayagyi U Ba Khin. The teacher admitted him to the retreat, then asked why he wanted to come. Goenka admitted he was trying to rid himself of migraines. In that case, the teacher said, you can't come. That would be a misuse of meditation, and it wouldn't work anyway. We sit to liberate ourselves, not for some personal medical reason.

Goenka agreed to subordinate his smaller purpose and joined the retreat for this larger one. He took to meditation and not only ended his migraines but eventually became a teacher, founding meditation centers all over the world. He put his business mind to good use.

Illness often marks that kind of turning point in a person's life. It gives us a chance to look at things more deeply.

Sometimes people equate physical health with spiritual development. They regard illness as a personal failure, a repudiation of one's life in the dharma. The assumption is that if we were living some kind of pure spiritual life we wouldn't be subject to illness. I remember that when Suzuki Roshi died of cancer at the age of sixty-seven, one of my students said rather casually that he couldn't have been an enlightened being if he died of cancer. On an even more ludicrous note, I once mentioned to a student that I was going to have a root canal, and I saw a look of shock and disappointment cross her face. I asked what was wrong, and she said, "How could this happen to someone with so strong a commitment to practice?"

The view of dharma is quite different. It sees the human body as an impermanent phenomenon like any other, one that not only will come to an end but also is constantly changing in unexpected ways. We have control over some conditions that affect the body but not others, and a part of wisdom is to know that. We need to take care of our bodies, but in a profound way we don't really own them, except in a conventional and legal sense.

A much more dharmic – and earthy – point of view is represented by the great teacher Ajaan Chah, who influenced many students in the West. He said, "Conditions all go their own natural way. Whether we laugh or cry over them, they just go their own way. And there is no knowledge or science that can prevent the natural course of things. You can get a dentist to look at your teeth, but even if he can fix them, they still finally go their natural way. Eventually even the dentist has the same problem. Everything falls apart in the end."

I am reminded of a story that the philosopher Huston Smith told journalist Bill Moyers about his stay at a Zen monastery in Japan. He had gotten interested in Zen in the middle of his life, so by the time he traveled to Japan he was somewhat older than the other men. The teachers made some concessions for him, but even so he found the rigors of a *sesshin*, an extensive period of intensive meditation practice, to be extremely difficult and – he felt – inhumane. The participants slept for only three hours per night and meditated long hours every day, in addition to doing hard physical work. The diet was spartan, mostly just rice, and totaled about nine hundred calories per day. It was a much more rigorous life than a middle-aged professor was used to living.

Smith got quite worked up – as newcomers tend to do – and finally stormed in to see the head monk. "This makes you angry," the monk said, smiling, and Smith said I *am* angry, and proceeded to detail just how inhumane the conditions were. "You probably think you'll get sick," the monk said, and Smith said, I *will* get sick, continuing his harangue. Finally the monk said, "What is sickness? What is health?" And that stopped the whole conversation. Smith understood the dualistic thinking that was behind everything he was saying.

This is not to say that there is no such thing as illness. Illness and health are useful classifications in our encounters with doctors. The problem is that we attach to these classifications as self; we see them as who we are. They separate us from experience and keep us from being intimate with our lives.

So there is sickness and there is health. But more specifically, there is always just how we are right now. That is what we practice with.

PRACTICING WITH HEALTH

I came to the spiritual path through yoga, and Shivananda Saraswati was my teacher at a time when I was growing interested in natural healing. This interest has become a part of my dharma practice but isn't shared by most of my fellow vipassana teachers. I take quite a bit of teasing about it, especially when I fall ill. "I just eat a lot of chocolate and cookies when I get sick," one of these teachers says, "and they make me feel better and help me heal more quickly. What's wrong with that?"

There's nothing wrong with it if it works for him. My interest is not in telling others how to live but in learning how to live myself and in using mindfulness to help me.

People tend to go to extremes in matters of health. The Buddha practiced for a while with ascetics who seemed to believe that the body – if not actually a hindrance – was at the very least unimportant, and they acted as if they wanted to do away with it, hardly nourishing themselves at all (the legend goes that, for a time, the Buddha subsisted on one grain of rice per day). He eventually, famously, decided that that was not the best way to practice, that a middle way was better.

Shivananda Saraswati encountered that same ascetic tradition in India, in Hindu monks who pay little attention to the body's health. It seems to me that all people, both secular and religious, who fail to consider their health are operating from that extreme. They neglect the body in the service of some supposedly higher endeavor. The body will sometimes take revenge for that neglect and behave as if it were an enemy.

At the other extreme – and this is an easy trap to fall into – are people obsessed with health. The Buddha spoke in his sutras of "the body within the body," by which he meant the moment-by-moment sensation of what is going on in the body, the constantly changing felt experience. But health fanatics can sometimes be obsessed with their body image, which can be an impediment to practice. They want to look slim, young, healthy, and radiant. They make their health concerns into another form of vanity, another kind of craving. They live as if they are their bodies. The language of some of the health magazines is positively militaristic: We've got to "combat" aging, "defeat" illness. But aging and illness will not ultimately be defeated.

Some of the yoga practiced today is what I sometimes call "leotard yoga," the practice that is motivated by a desire to have better abs, firmer thighs, and – above all – nicer buns. The hatha yoga that I practice is an ancient and venerable spiritual tradition. Its masters would be horrified to see yoga used for such petty concerns. Many contemporary health faddists see meditation – or some spiritual practice – as a minor adjunct to more important things, something to do "for a few minutes" each day, to make sure that your spiritual life is in shape too.

I never went that far, but some years ago I did get too caught up in caring for the body. It is a huge field of study, of course, and you can get more and more absorbed. I came to see the suffering of going overboard. And through the years I have become more accomplished in seeing that my interest in health doesn't get out of balance. It is important to realize that in this whole concern with health and wholeness of body and mind, wisdom should be in charge. Everything we do should come out of wisdom and go back to wisdom.

Illness Is Unavoidable

One of the people who reminded me of that fact was Chögyam Trungpa, the late renowned teacher of Tibetan Buddhism. I knew him when he first came to this country, before he had founded the centers and published the books for which he is now famous, and once had him come and talk to classes when I was still a professor. One day after class as we were walking across campus he suggested we have lunch. I told him I was fasting, a practice that I grew interested in through yoga and that I have continued to this day, with much benefit. He was intrigued and asked why I did that, so I tried to explain. Near the end of what I was saying he punched me hard in the back. "What do you want to do," he said, "live forever?" He had a point. I clearly needed someone to point out this preoccupation to me.

I can remember a time when all my caring for the body actually increased suffering for me around the fact of death. It seemed horribly sad to me that all the work I was doing, this beautiful functional body that I was creating, would eventually come to nothing. It didn't seem fair. But that was just an attachment like any other; I was attached to health.

The body is just one more thing that the fourth contemplation tells us we will eventually have to give up. Our task is to die to the body now, to see its impermanence and that we have only so much control over it, then to do the best we can. As long as wisdom stays in charge, it keeps us on track.

All of the questions that can be raised around health are just more occasions for mindfulness. There are plenty of prescriptions – eat only vegetables and fruits; eat a macrobiotic diet, and so on – and I have guidelines of my own, but such personal discoveries and preferences are not the subject of this book.

What amount of food and what kinds of foods do you need to feel your best? Some foods help the mind feel light and clear; others agitate and overstimulate us. Certain amounts of food enhance the mind's energy and clarity; others do not. How much exercise do you need to stay healthy and maintain mental clarity? How much sleep? The answers to these questions vary from person to person and from day to day for each person. Try different things and see how your body feels. The answers will probably also change as you age. You can never with finality sit back and say, Yes, I have health, because everything is constantly changing. Health is a matter of being attuned to how you are.

One ideal place to look into these questions is on retreat, where you have almost laboratory conditions set up to observe yourself. You are meditating a great deal and tend to be in touch with your body, so you can observe the effects of various kinds of food, various amounts of fluids, different kinds of walking.

The matter of food is especially interesting. At the Insight Meditation Society a buffet table of delicious vegetarian foods is laid out, and meditators have a chance to go through, select the right amounts, and eat mindfully. The conditions of silence often bring up people's issues about food, since they can watch closely what their minds do with it. It can be startling to see how often you use food for comfort and entertainment rather than just nourishment. Your observations can lead to changes in the way you eat back home.

Illness Is Unavoidable

People also face interesting issues about sleep on retreat. We pass long and somewhat strenuous days, starting at 5:00 AM and practicing until 9:00 at night. Many people, just out of habit, go to their rooms at that point and call it a day, passing up the optional evening sitting. But especially as the retreat goes on, people find that prolonged deep meditation produces energy rather than using it up. There are aches and pains in the early days, but by the fourth or fifth day people often notice they are tapping into reserves of energy. I encourage students to examine how they really feel and go back to the late-night sitting if they have some energy.

Sometimes staying up later is an expression of wisdom; at other times going to sleep is. Careful examination of your experience will show you. Your ability to discern correct action can be refined with practice. It isn't just a matter of sitting as much as possible. It is learning to see how you are, using mindfulness to show you how to live. When you go home at the end of the retreat, the same principles apply.

PRACTICING WITH PAIN

Retreats are also an ideal occasion to deal with pain, which often comes up on them and can be an excellent entrée into the larger subject of illness. Illness invariably involves *dukkha vedana,* the whole realm of unpleasant feelings. In facing illness, it is *dukkha vedana* that we must learn to deal with.

I need to introduce this subject carefully. Some people, hearing that on retreat we sit long hours in a cross-legged posture, that we raise pain – sometimes considerable amounts – and learn to observe it, think that our practice involves mortification of the flesh. That isn't the intention at all. There are meditation traditions where meditators are instructed not to move at all and someone yells at them if they do. Meditators may take a vow in the company of others not to move. There are traditions where meditators perform extraordinary feats – sitting from dusk until dawn, meditating for a week without sleep. I have experimented in many of these traditions, and they definitely have value.

But I don't teach in them, partly because I don't think they are healthy and partly because I feel a different kind of teaching is more effective in the long run. I instruct meditators to try to keep physical movement to a minimum – it's hard to develop concentration if you're moving around all the time – and if they do move, to do so mindfully. These instructions allow them to come along at their own pace, to gradually stay still for longer periods of time. But I do encourage them to deal with pain, to see if they can refrain from moving when it comes up and face it directly, dealing with it as a phenomenon.

For one thing, pain is a part of life. We spend a great deal of our lives chasing after pleasure and trying to avoid pain, and thereby create suffering for ourselves. A certain amount of pain in life is unavoidable, especially in conjunction with our larger subjects, sickness, aging, and death. If we stand and face it, instead of running away, we will handle it better.

The great Indian master Shantideva put it well. "There is

nothing whatsoever that is not made easier through acquaintance. So through becoming acquainted with small harms, I shall learn patiently to accept greater ones."

My first vipassana teacher, Anagarika Munindra, echoed that thought when I first asked him about practicing death awareness. I was especially concerned with how to practice as death draws close, because often at that time there are strong painful sensations in the body. He said, "It isn't necessary that you do anything new. The practice you're doing all along will get stronger and stronger, and when the time comes to die the task will be just the same, observing physical pain and seeing what the mind makes of it. It isn't essentially different. It's just a matter of strengthening the practice so that it is stronger than what comes in front of it, in this case the challenge of dying."

There is also a teaching on pain in the Pali canon. "On a certain occasion the Venerable Anuruddha was staying near Savatthi in a dark wood, being sick and grievously afflicted. Now, a number of monks came to visit him, and they asked, 'Pray, what is the Venerable Anuruddha's life in that the painful bodily feelings that arise do not affect his mind?' Anuruddha answers, 'Friends, it is because I dwell with my mind well grounded in the four foundations of mindfulness. That is why the painful bodily feelings that arise do not affect my mind."

The four foundations of mindfulness are a great teaching. They are really the basis of all vipassana meditation, a way of guiding the focus of our attention so that it may proceed in a comprehensive and systematic way. My own practice and

teaching are based on the presentation of these four foundations in the Buddha's *Anapanasati Sutra* (Full Awareness
with Breathing).

The first foundation of mindfulness is the body, practicing
mindfulness that is centered on the body; it can include the
breath as the object of attention. The second is sensations;
they are located in the body, but now we focus on whether
specific sensations are pleasant, unpleasant, or neutral. The
third foundation is the vast realm of the mind, the great
variety of mind-states, with special emphasis on the *kilesas:*
greed, hatred, and delusion. And the fourth is the realm of
wisdom, of vipassana practice per se, which involves a clear
and nonreactive seeing that all phenomena – the body sensations and mind-states – are constantly changing and are
not self.

All four foundations are involved in our observation of
pain. Pain takes place in the body, of course, but the mind
also tends to work on it, and the thing we finally notice if
we can stay with it long enough is that it is impermanent.
Most basically, however, pain is a phenomenon of the second
foundation. It is a form of *vedana* – bodily sensation – in
this case unpleasant sensation, or *dukkha vedana*. The question is: How do we handle that? How do we take care of
our pain?

We are back to the story of the two arrows: sensation and
the reaction to it. Pain is a wonderful way to illustrate it. Perhaps it would be helpful to include a fuller version of the story.
The Buddha is addressing his monks (the word in Pali is
bhikkhus, a term that includes all serious practitioners).

Bhikkus, people who do not know may feel pleasant sensations (sukha-vedana), unpleasant sensations (dukkha-vedana), and some neither-pleasant-nor-unpleasant sensations (that is, neutral, neither-sukha-nor-dukkha). Noble Disciples who already know may feel some pleasant sensations, unpleasant sensations, and some neither-pleasant-nor unpleasant sensations. Bhikkhus, in this case, what is special or strange, what is the difference between the Noble Disciples who know and those who do not?

Bhikkhus, the people who do not know, who are subject to the forces of unpleasant sensations, are sorrowful, mournful, crying and lamenting until they become deranged. They feel these two types of sensations – the physical and the mental.

It is like the hunter who shoots a person with one arrow and shoots yet another arrow into this same person. When this is the case, that person feels sensation due to both arrows – the physical as well as the mental. Those who do not know are just like this. . . . They feel two types of sensations, the physical and the mental. . . .

Bhikkhus, for those Noble Disciples who already know, when they feel the pangs of unpleasant sensations, they are not sorrowful nor mournful, they do not wail, lament, nor beat their breasts crying, nor do they become deranged. They feel only physical sensations, not mental torment.

It is like the hunter who shoots a person with an arrow and shoots yet another arrow that misses. When this is the case, that person will feel the sensations of only one arrow. The Noble Disciples who already know are like this. . . . They only feel physical pangs and remain unscathed by the mental ones.[1]

Let us imagine a meditator on a nine-day retreat. It is the second full day, often one of the worst for physical pain, and he is sitting right after lunch, often a time when energy is low. Our meditator has been having some trouble with his back, which is tired from the effort of sitting straight so many hours every day; toward the end of the morning it was starting to cramp up on him. Now he sits down, and at the very beginning of the sitting his back tightens up again. Before he knows it his mind has taken off.

"Not my back again! I was hoping that it would be better after lunch. I wonder how much time is left in this sitting. Practically the whole thing. I wonder how bad the pain is going to get. I don't think I can stand it if it gets much worse. How will I ever get through two more sittings this afternoon, to say nothing of two tonight? What if it just doesn't let up? What if it gets to a point where I can't stand it? What if I have to leave the room? What if I have to leave the retreat? Why did I want to come on this stupid retreat in the first place? Why did I ever take up meditating?"

And so on. The mind can go on this way for some time.

Clearly this is an example of the second arrow. Our meditator has started with a pain in the back and wound up – in

---

1. *Sallatha Sutta*, Samyutta Nikaya, XXXVI. 6

seconds, it seems – questioning his whole commitment to practice. It is possible as practice matures to watch the workings of the mind around pain. That can be most interesting and edifying. But a much more effective method is to focus on the pain itself.

A part of meditation practice is shifting the focus away from *this* and moving it to *that*. Though we cannot – as anyone who has meditated will tell you – stop the mind from thinking, we can shift the focus away from it. We can focus on the pain. And when we are concentrated on bodily sensations, the momentum of the thinking process is dramatically slowed. Attention directed at the body is energy not used for thinking.

Now we are back at the first arrow, the unavoidable one. Some physical pain is a fact of life. And though our first instinct is to resist, deny, or avoid it, what we typically find as we focus on it is that it isn't as bad as we might have thought. All our thinking, our identifying with the pain, was turning it into torment.

If you look closely you often notice some physical resistance to the pain as well as the pain itself. Muscles around the painful area are tensing in an effort to avoid it. But that tensing is itself a form of pain; sometimes the whole body grows tense, and wracked with pain, because of a small pain that started in the back or knee. If you are able to see that auxiliary tensing – especially if you can do so early on in the process – it often stops. Then you are back to the original pain, the original arrow.

You will notice that most thinking makes pain worse. As soon as your attention moves away, even for a few minutes, the pain intensifies. But everyone's attention wanders at first, and that is no reason to chastise yourself. The more you practice, the better you'll be able to stay with it. You begin to see that you're doing yourself a favor by staying focused on pain. It really isn't as bad if you can stay right with it.

It is important not to try to make it diminish, to use mindfulness to make it go away. That is just what everyone wants – to get rid of pain – and probably it won't work anyway. A corner of the mind is occupied with that yearning and is therefore separated from intimate contact with the pain. But it is intimacy that has transformative power.

Instead, you try to examine the phenomenon of pain very closely. In this case it is physical pain, but in some ways all pain is alike, and it all has a physical component. You are learning about pain through clear seeing, without having any ideas about it. There is no calculation, no scheming, no seeing pain as something to be transcended. You are examining it in the present moment.

And what you see, if you are able to stay concentrated for a long time, is that pain is a dynamic activity. We think of it as a solid fact – PAIN – but it isn't. It gets worse for a while, then it gets better. It might go away altogether, then come back with a vengeance. But it is not solid. And if you get really concentrated, go to subtler levels, you feel it as deep vibrations, more like a bundle or a stream of energy. This is another way of seeing its essential emptiness. Not only does it eventually end but it isn't solid when it's here. It isn't a substance with a core but is a process.

To really examine pain – or any other phenomenon – you

need to see it not just with mindfulness, *sati*, but with *sati-panna*, mindfulness with discernment. You need right effort to focus directly on the pain. You need right concentration to keep your attention focused. You need mindfulness to see the real flavor, the quality, of the pain. And you need discernment to see the impermanent and not-self nature of it. The pain arises and passes away and is not you. It is just pain.

Once you enter fully into pain, there is no "me" to suffer. There is just pain, which is observable and therefore work-able. What you're doing is a radical reexamination around the whole fact of pain, seeing that it is worth examining and stay-ing with. It's worth seeing what it really is.

When we deal with a phenomenon like pain, we are in a sense dealing with two kinds of time, two conceptions of time. One is what we can call psychological time, the time created by the thinking mind: the mind that wonders how long this pain will last, how much worse it will get, when it will ease up. That kind of time devours us. It is unrelenting and eats up our lives.

In contrast with that is what we might call absolute time, in which we are with things exactly as they are in the moment. We're not comparing them with how they were in a previous moment. We're not wondering how they'll be in the next mo-ment. We're just with them as they are. When we live that way, time doesn't devour us; we devour time. It is as if there were no time, because we are free from it. We are free from becoming.

Dogen expressed this concept with a striking metaphor in the *Genjokoan*.

Firewood becomes ash, and it does not become firewood again. Yet, do not suppose that the ash is future and the firewood past. You should understand that firewood abides in the phenomenal expression of firewood, which fully includes past and future and is independent of past and future. Ash abides in the phenomenal expression of ash, which fully includes future and past.[2]

I believe that this uniting with pain, this receiving it without separation, is also the best way to handle it, whether it is the pain of a long meditation retreat or of a serious illness. But some people, perhaps because their *samadhi* isn't yet sufficiently developed, can't do that, so I should mention some other ways to deal with it. One is just to focus on the breathing. This practice acknowledges the pain but admits that it is too much for the meditator at that particular time.

It is always an option to switch to the breathing when the pain becomes too severe, or when you tire of the effort of following it. If you can follow the pain, it is important to get back to it as soon as possible. It is that kind of clear seeing that will help you learn from it.

It is also possible to shift to a more panoramic focus. The pain is in your back, for instance, or your knee, so you widen your attention to the whole body, including breath sensations. You're not ignoring the pain; you're experiencing its existence as an integral part of the whole body. Such compre-

---

2. Kazuaki Tanahashi, ed., *Moon in a Dewdrop: Writings of Zen Master Dogen* (Berkeley, Calif.: North Point Press, 1995), p. 70.

hensive attention often has the effect of spreading out the sensations and making the pain easier to take.

I sometimes do advocate ignoring pain temporarily. You take the attention away from the part of the body that is hurting and focus on what doesn't hurt, then gradually return – when you feel able – to the center of the pain.

When students tell me they are unable to handle the extreme pain that comes up in sitting, especially on long retreats, I tell them they need to begin with smaller pains. Our daily life is full of little aches that are going on all the time and that we barely notice. If we bring them into focus, watching them arise and pass away, we not only will be more in touch with our daily lives but will also gradually develop the ability to focus on larger pains.

I also tell students, quite seriously, that you can never rest on your laurels with pain. Sometimes you have a sitting where you experience really severe pain, the worst you've ever had, and you're able to stay awake to it without reactivity and it passes. Then a few weeks or months later, a lesser pain comes up and you can't handle it. So much has to do with our energy and concentration in a particular moment. But there is always great worth in turning to our pain with fresh attention.

The most important thing is to realize that pain is a part of life. We put a great deal of energy into running from it, but that is a futile enterprise, because pain will catch up with us one way or another. Furthermore, we will face times in our lives – in serious illness and perhaps at the point of death – when pain is right there, when we will see quite clearly that our bodies and minds are out of our control. If we can learn early on how to work gently and decisively with pain, to be with it as it is, we will have a better chance to be present in those difficult situations.

Pain is the preeminent example of *dukkha vedana,* which often leads to great suffering, as it proliferates into complex mind-states. The sensation itself is the weak link in this chain of causation. If we can learn just to be aware of it with equanimity, we will avoid creating a great deal of unnecessary suffering.

Practicing with Illness

I have had two notable encounters with illness in my practice, and they both taught me a great deal. In both cases, teachers helped me, and without them I wouldn't have learned as much. These experiences came at different stages of my practice and taught me different things.

The first illness happened on a trip to Korea, and I can best explain it if I put it in context. After years of doing yoga and other kinds of awareness practice, I had decided I wanted to meditate seriously; I was all set to go to India to study when a friend told me he had found someone in the United States who could help me, a Korean Zen master named Seung Sahn, who taught in Providence, Rhode Island.

Zen Master Seung Sahn was an extremely charismatic, apparently fearless, and somewhat enigmatic man. He had been a Zen master in Korea and Japan, but when he first came to this country he worked as a washing machine repairman. In almost no time he gathered Zen students around him, and I was one of the most enthusiastic. I have always been grateful to him as my first Buddhist teacher; I learned much in my five intense years with him.

He seemed to know only about fifty words of English but had an amazing ability to make points with this limited vocabulary. He was a master of the dharmic sound bite. He was also a heroic, larger-than-life figure – the story goes that he had spent months meditating in caves, living on the food he could gather – and the Zen he taught was a high-energy heroic practice. We meditated on a koan, a question to ponder deeply – What am I? – and he would tell us, quite rightly, what an enormous undertaking it was. "Big question!" he would say. "What am I? *Big* question!"

It was with his example behind me that I went to Korea to live and practice for a year. By that time I had completely dedicated my life to practice. I had almost no money, but the laypeople would take care of me once I got to Korea, and some friends in Cambridge had contributed my round-trip airfare. To complicate matters even further, I had just started a promising relationship with a woman, and by going to Korea for a year I risked losing it (as it turned out, that is what happened). But I really wanted to seize this opportunity. I was on fire to practice.

But when I got to Korea, staying at Zen Master Seung Sahn's main temple in Seoul, I immediately got sick. The diet was rice, soup, vegetables, and pickled cabbage, even for breakfast, and I just couldn't hold the food. I had diarrhea for the first few weeks when I got there, got better for a while, then, when I went to a monastery up in the mountains for a retreat, got it again. I was extremely discouraged and also somewhat frightened. I'd experienced such stomach troubles in Mexico, but this was going on much longer than it had there. I had no money, didn't know what the medical care was like, and wondered if I'd ever get better. Worst of all, I had given up so much to come and practice, and I couldn't even do it. The whole thing seemed a waste.

The monk whom I had the good fortune to talk to at that moment was a ninety-six-year-old Zen master named Hae Am Sunim. He was small and shriveled and his legs didn't work anymore; he actually had to be carried out to meet me. But he still had a twinkle in his eye and a wonderful sense of humor. He understood my situation right away and set it right with a few words.

He addressed the energy I had for practice. "You want to ask *What am I?*" he said, speaking in a bold, booming voice, as Seung Sahn might have. "But all you can ask" – here he switched to a tiny, feeble, sickly voice, expressing just how I felt – "is *What am I?* That's fine. Ask that. When you are sick, practice like a sick person. When you get well you can ask the question like a lion again."

Hae Am Sunim was making an important point, for practicing with illness and for practicing in general. Dogen said the same thing in his instructions to the cook, when he told him not to worry about the ingredients he didn't have, just to work with those he did. At any given moment we are practicing with particular conditions, and one of them is the physical health we bring to the situation. It does no good to wish things were otherwise. A comparing mind brings suffering along with it. Just wholeheartedly use the ingredients you have, and don't worry about how things might have been. The last feeble breath you take, as you lie on your deathbed, will be a perfect one to follow. Weak energy is just as good to follow as strong.

My other experience of illness came years later and was much deeper, in part because I had been practicing much longer and also because I was now practicing vipassana meditation as taught in the Thai forest tradition. Zen concentrates on the big question, the big energy, and lets the little things go by. Vipassana meditation begins by focusing quite meticulously on small sensations. It concentrates on *vedana* until that practice itself becomes a deep source of insight.

Once again the circumstances were part of the story. I was traveling to Thailand to practice with the famous teacher Ajaan Maha Boowa, a student of Ajaan Mun, who had largely revived the Thai forest tradition. This was rather different from the collective practice I had done in Zen. We did get together in a hall to eat and do chanting, but we meditated mainly in *kutis* in the forest, little bamboo huts that were connected together by long paths. Meditators were alone in their *kutis*. We were near a small village, an overnight train ride from Bangkok, and a good distance from the nearest small city.

It is important to understand that the person undertaking this practice had been brought up in Brooklyn. They call it the Thai forest tradition, but I call it the Thai jungle tradition. A forest is where you go for a picnic, where the worst creatures you run into are ants and the worst catastrophe a rainstorm.

This was a lush tropical jungle, with snakes and all kinds of creatures slithering around, including a substantial community of rats who join meditators during the rainy season. There were even stories of monks encountering tigers during their evenings of walking meditation. The tigers were apparently gone, but the rats, insects, snakes, and wild chickens were plenty of company for me.

I had certainly been aware of the possibilities of illness and had brought a water purifier and lots of medicines, but within a few days I was sick in a way that made my Korean experience look like a walk in the park. I had a fever and terrible diarrhea and was vomiting. To make matters worse, I had bitten into a hard object in my food and broken a tooth. In Thailand the monks went to the village to beg for food, and we took what we got. I am normally a vegetarian, but I was eating chicken and fish. The food was actually quite good. But something was making me sick.

I was terribly discouraged. Once again I'd been extremely excited about going there to practice and instead I was spending much of my time lying down, when I wasn't running to the bathroom with diarrhea or running outside to vomit. I was also feeling a lot of fear. The conditions we were living in were quite primitive, and I seemed very ill.

Maha Boowa dealt with my anxiety first. He had a relaxed, jovial air and didn't seem at all worried. "Listen," he said. "You've taken all the medicines you have. You've taken all the medicines we have. It's time to let nature take its course. We don't think you're going to die. If we thought things were that serious, we'd find you the best medical help we could. This just seems to be the problem many Westerners have when they first come to Thailand."

Instead of letting this illness keep me from practicing, he said, I should practice with it. Forget about words like *dysentery, fever,* even *illness.* The sensations I was experiencing were as good for practice as any other. What I needed to do was focus on them and stay with them. It is when the mind wanders from its concentration that the difficulties arise. Suddenly it's *your* illness, these are *your* feelings, and you're full of self-pity. But when your concentration returns, they're just sensations again. He told me just to work with it, to see the impermanent nature of it all. The unpleasant sensations and the mind-states that accompanied them: All of them were empty. None was solid.

I told him that most of the time I couldn't sit. He said the physical posture was less important than the quality of the attention. I should sit when I could and at other times just practice in bed.

"Listen," Ajaan Maha Boowa said, "you're probably discouraged. Have you thought about going home?" I admitted I had. "You could do that," he said. "You could stay a week, then go back to the United States and talk at parties about your heroic week at the Thai forest monastery. But what would you have accomplished? Either way, the illness will run its course. But if you practice with it, you'll do something for your mind." He meant not my thinking mind but the larger realm of mind that we open up to when we meditate.

I don't think I could have done it without Maha Boowa's help, his calm, light-hearted encouragement to practice with my illness moment by moment. But with him there I was able to, and I can honestly say it was an extraordinary experience. My body was falling apart; I was spending much of my time in bed, but my mind was often positively blissful. Even as I was running to the jungle to throw up there was sometimes joy.

I probably wouldn't have had the conviction necessary to practice that deeply back in Korea, but in Thailand – with the help of Ajaan Maha Boowa – I did. The experience itself was wonderful, and Ajaan Maha Boowa told me it had other implications as well. "We don't know what is going to happen when it is time to die," he said. "But the skills you are learning now will help you then."

In my experience as a teacher I haven't found many students who practice with illness, even meditators with strong commitments, years of practice, and many retreats under their belts. These same people get sick and are out of commission for a while, and when they come back I ask, "Were you able to practice with your illness?" They look at me with blank stares. No, they say. They just lay around, watched television, and read. They were in some way equating practice with sitting. They were too tired to sit, so they felt they couldn't practice.

But times of illness – as Maha Boowa showed me – can be ideal times to practice. They are wonderful occasions to see the impermanence of the body.

Staying with the physical sensations, the moment-by-moment experience, is simply the best way to handle illness, when you can do it. But I also believe this practice helps the body heal. The mind and body are intimately connected, and when the mind runs off with all kinds of stories about what the illness may be doing to us – how it is a sign of aging, how it means we are near death – it causes greater tension. It is a kind of biofeedback mechanism that keeps energy from flowing and may actually impede the body's natural tendency to heal itself. So our mindfulness around illness may also help the body heal.

That possibility might account for the stories that come out of Burma about the remarkable healing powers of meditation, stories that were collected at the Mahasi Sayadaw Vipassana Center, in Rangoon. That is not a place devoted to healing; it is fiercely engaged in intensive practice and awakening. But they have kept records through the years, some showing cases of remarkable healings, even from tumors, strictly as a result of meditation. If we take all our scattered energies and bring them together in the practice of meditation, there is no telling what they can do.

That isn't *why* we meditate. It won't work if it is, because we won't really be meditating. And sooner or later, as the Buddha tells us, we all have to age, we have to face difficult and debilitating illness, and we have to die. Until that moment of death, anything that may arrive is food for practice. One of my teachers, Vimala Thakar of India, tells an inspiring story illustrating that fact, about a monk who insisted on practicing until the very end.

> I recall a moment in the life of an elderly saint whom I
> held in the highest esteem, saint Tukroji. He was suffer-
> ing from cancer. I went to see him in his ashram. He was

entirely illiterate. He knew as well as everybody else there that death was at hand. I had known since my childhood that he woke up at about three in the morning. He kept up the routine even when death was so near. He would tell the doctor and the nurse in perfect composure, "Put me in a sitting position, sponge the body, change the linen and the bedsheets, light up the lamp and the incense sticks. It is time now for me to go into meditation." And this went on until the end. I paid another visit to his room. The nurse helped him to sit up. He was a vaishnava devotee on Pandhari and in Maharashtra such a devotee puts some sandal paste on his forehead after he has taken his bath. And so he ordered the attendant to bring the sandalwood paste. When the unguents were brought, he asked the servant, "Where is the mirror? Do you think because I am going to die it will do if I put the mark on my forehead in any haphazard way I like? Do bring the mirror also. As long as I am alive I am thoroughly alive, and when I shall die, I shall die as thoroughly. At the moment I am very much alive and shall sing my prayer songs in full style." So he must have the mirror placed in front of him. He knew well enough that death was near. He knew the day and the time when it would arrive. There could not be a physical condition more critical than the one facing him at the time. He had shrunk to a mere skeleton. He would vomit blood. But what an air of grandeur was there in his manner when he said, "As long as I am alive I am fully alive. Put the mirror before me." And his grand manner as he put the sandal paste on his forehead was an entirely amazing sight.

It shook me to the roots. He would not neglect the present moment because the hour of death was approaching.[3]

---

3. Vimala Thakar, *Life as Yoga* (Delhi: Motilal Banarsidass, 1977).

ꙮ 3

THE THIRD MESSENGER
Death Is Unavoidable

In brief, without being mindful of death, whatever Dharma
practices you take up will be merely superficial.

— MILAREPA

I am subject to death. Death is unavoidable.

THE Cambridge Insight Meditation Center hosted Tara
Tulku Rinpoche some years ago. Before he gave a talk he
would finger the beads that some Tibetans carry and make a
certain sound three times. I thought he must be intoning
some special mantra. Finally I asked him about it and he said
he was repeating a simple phrase: "I'm going to die. I'm going
to die. I'm going to die." The idea was that those words would
keep him from any inflated ideas he might have of being a
teacher or some kind of expert. All of his supposed expertise
and authority would come to nothing.

I keep various mementos around to remind me of the same
thing. One is the skull of a dead lama. Another is a set of beads
made from the bones of a dead lama. It was taken from the remains of a corpse after what is called a sky burial, in which

vultures are allowed to consume a corpse as a last act of compassion. And the beads that Tara Tulku Rinpoche fingered as he said those words were also made of bone. Beads made of human or animal bones serve as a reminder of how we're all going to end up.

People often ask why we would want to be reminded. It's bad enough that we have to die: Why remind ourselves of that fact all the time? The Pali word *anusaya* refers to the latent tendencies that we all have, one of which is our fear of death. It lives in our consciousness somewhere and weighs us down, actually having quite a bit of influence on us, as it shows up in smaller, more tangible fears. It darkens our lives. It is a chronic form of anxiety.

Anusaya is constantly fed by things we see and hear: when someone we know dies, or when we see a dead animal in the street, or when we hear that a friend has grown seriously ill or see a friend after some time and notice that he has aged. The way of Buddhist practice is to flush out these fears, to open the doors and windows and let in some fresh air, to stop talking about these matters in a whisper, repressing and denying them. It's exhausting to live that way; it requires a huge amount of energy to hold that kind of fear down. And it doesn't ultimately work.

One thing we may find as we begin to penetrate this subject is that we're not really afraid of dying; we're afraid of the idea of dying. This sounds like an overly subtle distinction, but it's an important one. When death actually comes it will be a moment like this one, an experience like any other, which we will try to stay awake for. Our body and our breathing will feel a certain way; particular things will be coming up in our mind. But right now, looking ahead to death we have elaborate ideas about dying, which probably bear little relationship to the experience we will actually go through.

It is like many other experiences in life; the anticipation is worse than – or at least different from – the actual event. In the practice of death awareness, what we are trying to do is arrive at a place that is beyond thought, because it is thought that creates so many of our problems. We don't actually know what lies beyond death. Death is the great unknown, and thought – which is an expression of what is known – cannot know the unknown. There is nothing deep about that; it is just a fact. We call it the unknown because we don't know.

If fear comes up at the thought of death, I'm all for that; it is our fears that we contact intimately. But the cascading thoughts we have as those fears arise are not of much use. And in contemplating death, we are not trying to get beyond any knowing that we might have right now. We are just trying to be with what is here now. Death is here now.

This is the subject that the others have all been leading to. Buddhism's most basic teachings have to do with impermanence and change. Aging and sickness are aspects of change. They are perfectly natural. Death, too, is perfectly natural. The body wears out over time, sometimes – depending on circumstances – a short time, sometimes a longer time. Finally it gives out altogether.

However, even though these are the facts of our lives, and though we will all have to face them sometime, the contemplation of death is not for everyone at any particular moment.

Death Is Unavoidable

If this is a time in your life when things have been difficult, if you've endured some recent losses, if you're going through a period of depression, it might not be a good time to take up the practice of death awareness. (And likewise, please be sensitive with your friends and loved ones who are facing death themselves – the deathbed is *not* the place to introduce them to this kind of practice, especially if they don't have much experience of the dharma.)

It does help if you've been practicing for a while, if you've established a certain degree of *samadhi*. But I have also found, in practice groups through the years, that even people who haven't developed much *samadhi* are able to take up a simple statement like "I must die" and concentrate on it well, because the subject itself generates great interest. You don't want to take it up if it stimulates a kind of fear that you are not able to handle. But you don't necessarily need to be an advanced meditator.

For someone who does feel ready, the practice of death awareness can be invaluable. We are priming the pump, flushing out fear, inviting it to appear so we can get to know it in an intimate way. And what we invariably see about our fears is that they are impermanent. However difficult they may seem, they have a limited life span: they arise, exist for a while, and pass away. The energy of fear is there, but it is not me or mine. It is not self.

Once we have seen that, we take a great deal of the power out of our fears. They are no longer lurking half acknowledged in our consciousness. They have lived out their lives. And though they may return, we have a newfound confidence that we can handle them. We've seen that our fears are observable and therefore workable.

It is in that way that these reflections enhance our appreciation of life. They actually remind us of how precious life is. They let us see life in all its beauty, because we are acknowledging that it will end. We have voluntarily walked into the house of death. And we see that we have been living in a kind of fool's paradise. We have been pretending life will go on forever. We therefore haven't seen its fullness and its splendor.

We know in our heads that we will die. But we have to know it in our hearts. We have to let this fact penetrate our bones. Then we will know how to live.

To do that, we need to be able to look at the fact of death with steadiness. We can't just glance at it casually. All of our training in dharma practice is preparation for such deep seeing. Taking the refuges and ethical precepts, which is a traditional first step; working with the breath – which can be a long process – to develop a calm and concentrated mind; working with sensations, with small fears and progressively larger ones; developing mindfulness in everyday life: All of these steps work together to build a mind that is strong enough to look at the fear of death. Sometimes, before we are able to observe this fear directly, we need to learn how to be with our resistance to it. We are mindful of how much we hate to have fear in the first place.

If you haven't done this preparatory work, you probably aren't going to be ready to look at death. There may be a few exceptional individuals who can, who just seem to arrive on the earth with remarkable spiritual maturity or who have perhaps had life experiences that develop that maturity. But most of us need to work at it. We need to develop a mind that is capable of looking at things with some steadiness, so we can stay with them long enough for the message to come through. Communing with fear stimulates an understanding that has liberating power.

Typically, our awareness is sporadic. We might be watching the evening news and hear of some tragedy, and we notice a momentary pang or a real feeling of heartsickness. But something else comes on the screen, or we move on to some other activity, and it's over. That's the way of the modern world. Short brief bursts of attention.

Our practice is different. The *samadhi* we develop is not a rigid concentration, which shuts things out. The mind that develops *samadhi* is strong and supple, very much alive. The state we develop is more like tenderness. The heart begins to melt. You see the true sorrow of life and its true beauty. You can't see one without the other. Practice opens us up to both.

Sometimes when your heart grows tender from practice, a single event touches it in such a way that you are suddenly more awake: You see deeply into the nature of things. Then everything becomes more precious, all the people and all the surroundings of your life. Your urge to intensify meditation practice can grow as well.

I don't mean something narrow by *practice,* that you quit your job and leave your family to go off and meditate in a cave somewhere. I mean it in a broad sense: You stay awake in everything you do. You make the practice a vital part of your entire life. And when you learn to practice with ordinary events, you are capable of staying with the extraordinary ones. Like the moment of death.

I have learned a great deal from the teachings of Zen master Suzuki Shosan, a meditator who had also been a samurai and who had even put in some time as a hermit. He had been fiercely trained in combat. His teaching was to use death awareness, or, as he put it, "death energy," to stimulate his practice. When problems came up in his life, he would use death energy to reorchestrate the conditions, and it proved to be a great help.

"If you yourself can die gladly," he said, "you will have become a buddha. Buddhahood is to die with an easy mind." He goes on, with painful honesty: "Because I am a man who does not want to die, I practice in order to be able to die freely. Freely stretching out my neck for the executioner without a thought."

He is using the executioner as a symbol of death. He means that when the time comes, he hopes to surrender to death gracefully. "I've trained myself in various ways," he says, "and I know the agony of not dying freely. My method is a coward's Buddhism." We are all cowards, in that sense. We all need some kind of training.

Some of the deepest learning about death is not formal, of course; it comes about naturally when – for instance – one's parents die. But you learn from such an event only if you really look at it, as you would in more formal practice. If you're open to the experience, every person who dies is your teacher.

I feel that my father's last gift to me was that he taught me I was going to die. I'm not exempt from the law he was subject to. I have had moments in my life when it seemed unthinkable that my father would die, this man who for many years seemed bigger and stronger than I and whom I modeled myself on when I was growing up. But he did die, and he's not coming back. Ashes do not become wood again. Someday I too will be ashes.

PRACTICING FORMALLY

These thoughts about my father actually begin to move us into more formal death awareness practices. I have used – and taught – a nine-part meditation that has been adapted from the teaching of Atisha (980–1055), the great Indian Buddhist sage. I have modified these contemplations with personal instructions from Tara Tulku Rinpoche and Ajaan Suwat. They are the basis of the death meditation that I teach today.

This practice is divided into three general topics: the inevitability of death, the uncertainty of when you will die, and the fact that nothing but the dharma can help you at the time of death. Each category includes three contemplations.

In a typical session, it is a good idea to begin with breath awareness, giving the breath exclusive attention until the mind settles down. Once you have reached some calm, you are ready to take up a contemplation like the first one: Everyone must die.

Obviously, this contemplation requires a concentrated mind. There is no fact of human existence that we are more likely to want to escape. We naturally have great aversion to it, and when our capacity to pay attention is limited, the true significance of the contemplation does not penetrate to the heart. But in a serene mind, thinking can be sharp and pliable. We can direct our attention with precision and focus, and our reflection can be uninterrupted. It has the powerful support of *samadhi,* which enables us to stay emotionally engaged and keenly interested.

If we just turn the contemplation over in our mind, the richness of its meaning reveals itself. We stay attentive to our experience as it tells its story and allow the truth of the contemplation to affect us. We experience it not just with our thinking mind but with our entire being. These nine reflections of Atisha are an exercise in *yoniso manasikara* – careful concentration. Any of these simple verbal statements when attended to in a thorough and sustained way can take us beyond their surface meaning. Probing these statements deeply can help us uncover the workings of the natural law of dharma in our own bodies and minds.

In a given session, you might give your primary focus to a particular contemplation, then briefly review the other eight, to remind yourself of them. You might choose to do one contemplation per day, or perhaps all three within a particular heading. If a given contemplation seems fruitful, you might want to stay with it for a number of days. All of these contemplations get at the same basic truth, and your practice with them need not be rigid. You can use your innate wisdom to decide how best to work with them.

All of this will become clearer as we move into specific examples.

Death Is Unavoidable

THE INEVITABILITY OF DEATH

1. *Everyone must die.*

The first – and boldest – of these contemplations is that everyone and everything must die. No one escapes this inevitable law. Death is a logical consequence of birth and begins to work on life at the moment of birth. There are no exceptions. Differences in wealth, education, physical strength, fame, moral integrity, even spiritual maturity, are irrelevant. If you don't want to die, don't be born.

Buddhaghosha's *Visuddhimagga* is of some help here. It suggests that you compare yourself with others of great fame, merit, supernatural powers, deep understanding. The Buddha died. Jesus Christ. Socrates. Great and famous athletes: the strongest men and women in the world, the fastest, those capable of the most extraordinary physical feats.

Krishnamurti is someone whom I often contemplate in this way. It is helpful if you have actually known the person. He had incredible inner strength and clarity and immense vitality, which I experienced in his presence over a period of many years. He taught until several weeks before he died at the age of ninety. But he did die.

You can also take up ordinary people who have seemed extremely vital and alive. Probably we have all known someone who seemed absolutely irrepressible and unstoppable. That person, too, is subject to death.

Sometimes methods just suggest themselves. One night some years ago I had given a talk on death awareness, so it was on my mind afterward when I went up to my apartment to unwind. I love movies, especially old ones. That night there was a film from 1938 with Clark Gable and Carole Lombard, and as a film buff I had heard of everyone who was involved, the writer, the director, the producer. Suddenly I realized that everyone connected to that movie was dead.

There they were bounding around in the prime of life, wonderfully virile and sensual and attractive. And all of them were dead. The person who got the idea, the person who fleshed it out and wrote the screenplay, the person who wrote the score, everyone who played in the orchestra. Probably even the people who sold the popcorn in the theaters were dead. It was stunning to realize. The movie was so alive, and they were so dead.

The Buddha put it this way:

> Young and old,
> foolish and wise,
> rich and poor, all keep dying.
> As a potter's clay vessels,
> large and small, fired and unfired,
> All end up broken,
> so too life leads to death.[1]

2. *The remainder of our life span is decreasing continually.*
Our movement toward death is inexorable. It never stops. From the moment we're born, we are dying. Death comes closer with every tick of the clock. The great Indian master

---

1. *Mahaparinibbana Sutta*, Digha Nikaya 16.

Atisha used the sound of water dripping as a way to practice this contemplation.

We can use a variety of objects. One of the simplest – and best – is the breath itself. We have only a finite number of breaths in our life – it may be a rather large number, of course, and we have no idea what it is – and with each breath we use up another. Every breath brings us closer to death.

This is part of the real depth of breath awareness, the place where it can take us. We start out thinking we're watching a simple physical function, but the more we do it, the more we realize what a profound phenomenon we're observing. Each inhalation, after all, is a tiny bit of life; it is bringing air into the lungs, oxygen into the body, and allowing us to live. Each exhalation is a letting go, a releasing. At some point we will exhale and not inhale again. And our life will end.

We can contemplate the breath in exactly that way, releasing each exhalation with no certainty or even expectation that there will be another breath. Especially when we have been sitting for a while, the breath can grow very deep, and there can be a long pause between exhalation and inhalation. It can be a moment that is fraught with anxiety. Sometimes we finally force an inhalation, just to assure ourselves that we will breathe again. But the more we sit, the more we are able to let the process just happen and stay with the moment between breaths, when we are not sure we will breathe again.

Such a practice can sound terrifying. We might be arousing one of our primal fears – the fear that we will not be able to get our breath – which is behind many of our other, smaller fears. And whatever the contemplation calls up – fear, terror, hysteria – that is what we practice with. We stay with it, letting that fear exist alongside the process of the breath itself, and see that it too is an impermanent phenomenon, that it is workable.

Such a fear is very much like physical pain. If we turn away from it or run from it, it looms larger and larger and can become really difficult. But if we stay with it, we see first of all that it isn't as bad as we might have thought. Then we see that it comes to an end. Our whole relationship to fear – and to breathing – can change in that moment. Seeing impermanence helps decondition the mind's strong tendency to grasp and cling.

Sometimes, of course, we sit down expecting fear to come up, expecting some violent reaction, and nothing happens. Or maybe fear arises briefly and doesn't continue. We keep turning the contemplation over in our minds with no result. That's all right. We can't control such things and can never be sure when our emotions will engage. We don't want to force anything or have the feeling we're trying to break through to something. We just want to be present with the experience we are having.

In any case, the second contemplation concerns our steadily decreasing remaining days. It is as if we have fallen from a tree in the dark of night. We know we're going to hit the ground at some point. We just don't know when.

The seventh Dalai Lama expressed it in a poem.

> After our birth we have no freedom to remain even
>   for a minute.

> We head towards the embrace of the Lord of Death,
>   like an athlete running.
> We may think that we are among the living, but our life
>   is the very highway of death.[2]

*3. Death will come regardless of whether or not we have
made time to practice the dharma.*
This contemplation focuses on the fact that our major reason
for contemplating death is to spur us on to practice. I assume
in that statement a basic commitment to meditation practice,
and I may be assuming too much. I am, after all, a meditation
teacher. It may be that another kind of person confronting the
harsh reality of death might give up his job and opt for a life of
sex, drugs, and rock and roll. Who knows?

But this contemplation is letting us know that time is precious and we have little of it. We all spend countless hours
sleeping, eating, just hanging around. Not that those things
aren't important. But we have to ask ourselves how we want to
spend what precious little time we have.

We have all probably asked ourselves: What would I do if I
had just one more year to live? It is an interesting question,
and we all hope we have more than that, but we definitely have
a limited time. How do we want to spend it? To what do we
want to devote our lives? It's a question we need to ask.

As a dharma teacher, I frequently meet people who are

---

2. Gyalwa Kalzang Gyatso (seventh Dalai Lama), "Meditations on the Ways
of Impermanence," in *Living in the Face of Death*, Glenn H. Mullin (Ithaca,
N.Y.: Snow Lion Publications, 1998).

wrestling with this contemplation. "As soon as I get my degree, I'm really going to practice." "When I finish my novel . . ." "When I close one last business deal . . ." "When my children are grown . . ." Gungtang Rinpoche summed up this mind-set well:

> I spent twenty years not wanting to practice dharma. I spent the next twenty years thinking that I could practice later on. I spent another twenty years in other activities and regretting the fact that I hadn't engaged in dharma practice. This is the story of my empty human life.

What is really needed here is a change in priorities, as well as a change in attitude. Almost all of us have circumstances in our lives that make practice somewhat difficult. And when people make these excuses to me, they are mostly talking about finding more time for daily sitting practice, more time to do all-day sittings and longer retreats. These things are extremely valuable and important. But the real question is: Do we dare to practice, to commit ourselves to practice, right now? The whole of our lives is a wonderful field for practice. Can we use it? The simplified, protected situation of formal sitting practice is invaluable, but can we also practice while we are raising our children, going to school, going to work, writing a novel, even driving the car or going to the bathroom? The mind-set that sees certain periods of time as available for practice and others not is mistaken from the outset. All of us can practice, with everything we do. It is just a question of whether or not we dare to do it.

When people approach practice in that way, when they

bring it into their daily lives, what often happens is that they see benefits from it, and their practice catches fire, and suddenly time for sitting practice looks different. When they come to understand that sitting is the real basis of practice, it is amazing how time suddenly shows up for it. It almost happens by itself.

So the first thing people need to face is not a scheduling conflict. It is whether or not they want to give themselves to practice. When students do that, the time shows up by itself.

This contemplation faces that question directly: To what will we give the days of our lives?

The Uncertainty of the Time of Death

4. *Human life expectancy is uncertain.*
A graveyard is a wonderful place to practice this contemplation, especially an old one. Just walk around and look at the headstones and see at what age people died. But sometimes an old graveyard gives us a false sense of security; we think that since the discovery of antibiotics and of various vaccines, because of all our recent medical advances, things have changed. They have; the average life expectancy is longer. But people still die at all ages. Just read your newspaper. Watch CNN. Talk to your neighbors. You'll hear all kinds of stories.

This contemplation really just reflects the law of impermanence. A corollary of that law is that change happens in unexpected ways. It would be one thing if all phenomena changed predictably. It might still be difficult, but at least it would have a pattern. But the truth is that life can snatch the rug out from under us. The floor can cave in. So can the roof. And we never know when such an event might happen.

It isn't just death that is uncertain but also life. We all want permanent things: a permanent partner, a permanent job, a permanent family, house, income, group of friends, place to practice meditation. Permanently good weather. We do everything we can to assure permanence in all of these areas; we spend all our time trying to assure ourselves, and it never works. Nothing is permanent. We would spend our time much more wisely by contemplating and absorbing the law of impermanence rather than trying to repeal it. If we could learn to really live with it, our lives would be much different.

It is like the story of a famous sage who was asked where all his wisdom came from. He replied, "I live as a man who, when he wakes up in the morning, does not know if he will be alive when the day ends." His questioners were puzzled. Isn't that true of everyone? they asked. "It is," he said, "but few people live that way."

The law of impermanence is not good news or bad news. It isn't even news. It is just a fact, the most obvious fact in the universe. But we live as if it weren't true, or as if it allowed exceptions. Impermanence is like the law of gravity, which operates on us whether we like it or not.

Again, the seventh Dalai Lama wrote a poem on this subject, about men going into battle.

> Spirits were high with expectations this morning,
> As the men discussed subduing enemies and protecting
>   the land.

> Now, with night's coming, birds and dogs chew their
> corpses.
> Who believed that they themselves would die today?[3]

While I was giving the talks on which this book is based, an American Zen master I knew fell over dead of a heart attack in the middle of an interview. He was in his early fifties. My writing partner decided not to move but to renovate his present house largely because he loved his neighbors; in the middle of the renovations, everyone's favorite neighbor – the man they called the mayor of the street – was diagnosed with a brain tumor, and within months he was dead.

Everyone has stories like these. Just look at today's obituaries. Many of these people were elderly; many had been ill. But how many really expected they would die when they did? We hear of such things happening to other people and think it will never happen to us, but chances are that it will, one way or another. It is often true that when death finally comes, it is not expected.

5. *There are many causes of death.*
It seems to be a peculiarly modern problem that we think we can find a cure for everything, solve any problem. We licked polio; we eliminated smallpox; we don't have thousands in sanitariums with TB anymore; and now we want to cure everything else. We put tremendous time and energy into seeking cures for AIDS and for various kinds of cancer, and of

---

3. Gyalwa Kalzang Gyatso, "Meditations on the Ways of Impermanence."

course these are worthy projects. But we can get into a mind-set where we think we're going to cure everything. We're going to eliminate death.

The fact is that we eliminate one thing and another comes up. We no longer die of consumption, but now there's AIDS. We do much better fighting some forms of cancer, but with others – despite all kinds of sophisticated treatment – we are not successful. Remissions occur, but then the cancer comes back. And we need to remember also that in large parts of the world many diseases haven't been eliminated at all. People still die from things that killed us in this country eighty or a hundred years ago but no longer do. Malaria, for instance, is still the number one killer in the world.

And that is just illness. It says nothing of war, famine, murder, suicide, car accidents, accidents of other kinds, hurricanes, avalanches, floods, earthquakes, tornadoes, drownings. We could go on and on. If we find a way to eliminate all the illnesses we currently face, others will arise, because the earth can support only so many people, and it will take care of itself. And sooner or later the earth itself will die. It is an impermanent phenomenon like any other, with a beginning, middle, and end.

To be alive, then, is to be subject to any number of causes and conditions, some of which come upon us unexpectedly and have unexpected results. To feel protected from these things is to be living in a fool's paradise. We have just been temporarily spared.

As Nagarjuna said, "We maintain our life in the midst of thousands of conditions that threaten death. Our life force abides like a candle flame in the breeze. The candle flame of our life is easily extinguished by the winds of death that blow from all directions."[4]

At about this point in the contemplations, we begin to feel that the whole thing is senseless, that these contemplations are the concoction of a wicked and morbid imagination and that if we listen to them any more we'll be too depressed even to live. So it is good to pause here with a word of warning: Of course this view of things is morbid and depressing, overwhelming when presented all at once, and of course there are many wonderful things in life. The fact that life is impermanent and uncertain does not mean that it is worthless. Seen correctly, these facts make life more precious. They show us that every moment is a gift.

The point of these contemplations is to correct an imbalance. We all live, too often, as if these facts of life don't exist. These contemplations on death are intended to wake us up. They awaken us ultimately to the joy and beauty of a life free of craving and grasping, a life where we see through the illusion of being young and healthy forever and drop it.

6. *The human body is very fragile.*
I had an uncle who died at the age of twenty-two. He was slicing vegetables with a rusty knife and accidentally cut himself. Within a few days he was dead.

A son of President Warren Harding apparently died be-

---

4. Jeffrey Hopkins, *Buddhist Advice for Living and Liberation: Nagarjuna's "Precious Garland"* (Ithaca, N.Y.: Snow Lion Publications, 1998).

cause he neglected a blister and got blood poisoning. In North Carolina this summer, a huge hulking football player in wonderful physical condition – a star of the team and president of the senior class – got overheated during practice despite many precautions by his coaches. His body temperature went up to 107 degrees and the emergency medical workers couldn't get it down. He died soon after he got to the hospital.

So on the one hand the human body is enormously resilient. We have all heard stories of people who endure tremendous hardships during wars or natural disasters, or who are old and sick and seem to hang on forever. On the other hand, the body is terribly vulnerable. A microbe can kill it. A hard blow to a fragile organ can. A cut to a key artery. Death can come very quickly.

The import of all three of the contemplations in this category is the same. It isn't to scare us, though fear may come up. It isn't just to make us more careful, though it may help us take our days less for granted. The point is that we all tend to see life following a certain pattern. We imagine youth, a long period of adulthood, and a serene old age, at the end of which we peacefully expire.

That is just an idea. It is an image. Death isn't waiting for us at the end of a long road; it is with us every minute. Our lives are impermanent and fragile, our fate uncertain. The intention of these contemplations is to make that fact vivid, to call it up before us and make us see things as they really are. Whichever contemplation does that best for you is the one to use.

Death Is Unavoidable

Only the Practice of Dharma
Can Help Us at the Time of Death

7. *Our wealth cannot help us.*

The last set of contemplations is an extremely rich one for dharma practitioners. It is in some ways a minute examination of the fourth contemplation from our earlier group: "I will grow different, separate from all that is dear and appealing to me." It can be an extremely effective, if difficult, set of exercises.

What I would encourage you to do is actually picture yourself on your deathbed. Settle into a period of meditation, establish some *samadhi,* then do a visualization. Imagine yourself in your room, with a clear mind, waiting for the moment of death. Imagine what you might be thinking and feeling.

Wealth is a kind of shorthand in this first contemplation. Few of us think of ourselves as wealthy (though the fact is that, compared with most people from the past and in the rest of the world, we live in almost unimaginable luxury), but we all have things, we probably all have some cherished things, and we might have spent a lifetime working to accumulate them. Our book collection. Our record or CD collection. A beloved musical instrument. Our car. Our clothes. Our house. Think of all we have done to acquire these objects, especially those that we craved for a long time.

I'm not saying there is anything wrong with such possessions. But none of them can help you at the moment of death. Pick up your favorite book, your musical instrument, your suit or dress. Your statue of the Buddha. You will have to give them all up and will never see or touch any of them again. These objects can't ward off death or make the experience more manageable.

If that is the true reality of life and death, and if dharma practice could be of some help to you – as it is certainly my feeling that it could – wouldn't it have been better to give more of your time to practice and less to accumulating objects that are going to turn to dust in your hands?

Tara Tulku Rinpoche pointed out to me that Americans – who pride themselves on being shrewd, hard-nosed business-men – are actually bad businessmen. They're not watching the bottom line at all. They are putting all their energy into something ephemeral and ultimately unfulfilling. Even your good name, your spotless reputation, all your accumulated learning, your prizes and awards, your tenured position, will not accompany you where you're going now. Why did you spend so much time earning them?

One can't help thinking of the wealthy young man in the Bible who approached Jesus. He asked what he could do to find eternal life. And Jesus – clearly seeing what was holding this particular person back – said, Give up all that you have and follow me. The young man walked sorrowfully away. He couldn't bring himself to do that. But sooner or later we will all have to do it. It is just a matter of time. We are clinging to things that cannot last.

Krishnamurti delivered this message quite clearly: The reason that death is so hard for you is that your life has been about attachment and accumulation. "Do you want to know how to die?" he said. "Think of the thing you treasure the most and drop it. That is death."

> Avoid works of little consequence;
> And seek the path to spiritual joy.
> The things of this life quickly fade;
> Cultivate that which benefits eternally.
>
> —DUL ZHUG LING

8. *Our loved ones cannot help.*
This contemplation is the most difficult one for many people. We can see that our book collection, our music, our good reputation and our titles, our position in the community, all might have some ego in them. It might be that our devotion to them is slightly misguided. But we think our human relationships are not tainted in that way. Our relationship to our spouse or partner. Our parents. Our children. Brothers and sisters. Close friends. Our spiritual teachers. We believe we have some relationships that have a certain purity to them.

That may be true. But it is also true that our friends cannot help us when we die. They may be there (and they may not; we don't know how that will go). They may comfort us. But in the end we have to say good-bye to them and not see them again. We have to die alone. As Shantideva said:

> While I am lying in bed, although surrounded by all my friends and relatives, the feeling of my life being severed will be experienced by me alone. When I am seized by the messengers of the Lord of Death, what benefits will my friends afford? What help can my relatives be? At that

time the sole thing that will provide me with a safe direction will be the degree of purity of my mind-stream. But have I ever really committed myself wholeheartedly to such cultivation?[5]

I don't know of any visualization that can make the truth of death more real to you. Picture yourself lying on your deathbed. Imagine the person whom you love most in the world coming to your side. Then imagine yourself saying good-bye to that person forever.

That is the reality of death. For most people, it is the most difficult part.

It is only natural to turn to those we love at the time of death. But despite our close bond with those people, we must finally die alone. Strong attachments only make matters worse; our departure will be marked with torment. Grasping and peace don't go together. We come into the world alone and must leave it alone.

9. *Our own body cannot help.*

We are really getting close to home. We have just said good-bye to the person who is nearest and dearest to us. Now we must say good-bye to our own body.

Throughout our lives, our body has been our closest companion. At times it has seemed to be who we are. We have spent hours washing and cleaning and clipping and oiling and

---

5. Shantideva, *A Guide to the Bodhisattva's Way of Life*, translated by Stephen Batchelor (Dharmasala, India: Library of Tibetan Works and Archives, 1992).

combing and brushing, taking care of our body in all kinds of ways. We have fed it and rested it. We might have had differing attitudes toward it, sometimes loving it and sometimes hating it. But now this closest companion, which has gone through everything with us, will no longer be here. It will no longer take in oxygen. It will not circulate blood. This body that for so many years was so full of vitality will be lifeless. It will be a corpse.

The first Panchen Lama says it well: "This body that we have cherished for so long cheats us at the time when we need it most."

It is also true that this will not be the last change it will undergo. As a physical phenomenon, the dead body, if not cremated, will decompose, and it is common in Buddhist practice to consider the stages of change and decay in order to bring the reality of death home.

Buddhist monks sometimes actually visit the charnel grounds to contemplate these other forms, to see our final fate, and there is a whole series of charnel ground meditations as well. The *Mahasatipatthana Sutra,* the Buddha's main teaching on what to be mindful of in meditation, offers some guidelines as to how to practice with dead bodies at various stages of decomposition. For our purposes, visualization of these stages is more practical.

As with the earlier contemplations, we first calm the mind with breath awareness; then through words and visualizations we create each stage and contemplate it. It is important to make a connection between the image and our own body. One traditional formulation is: "Truly, my body is of the same nature as the body being visualized. It won't go beyond this nature. It is of the same lawfulness." Our bodies don't belong to us but to nature. And nothing in nature has a stable form.

Reflecting in this way helps us come to terms with the nature of the body. We view it with wisdom, see that it can't be any other way. If fear or resistance comes up, we see that too with nonjudgmental awareness, watching it arise and pass away.

Ajaan Suwat taught me a version of this practice that I found extremely helpful. In his approach, you would start out by visualizing an inner organ of the body that you can easily picture, then watch what happens to it after death as the body goes through its stages of decomposition. When you reach the ninth contemplation (listed below) – when everything is ashes and dust – visualize it re-forming to its starting point. Finally – and I found this crucial – focus on the mind that is aware of all this. See that it is completely separate. This understanding keeps the charnel ground contemplations from becoming overwhelmingly depressing.

Both of my parents instructed me to have them cremated when they died. My father died first, and I placed his picture and the urn with his ashes on the home altar where I meditate each day. In addition to my daily vipassana practice, I would find some time in most sittings to look at his picture and remind myself that the urn contained all that was left of his body and that I was not exempt from the same process. Such reflections sometimes aroused a powerful sense of how unstable my body is.

Death Is Unavoidable

As I write these words, my mother's ashes now rest in an urn on the same altar. I am carrying out the same practice with her, and it is proving to be equally rich. Such teaching is the last gift that my extraordinarily generous parents were able to give me.

CHARNEL GROUND MEDITATIONS FROM THE
Mahasatipatthana Sutra[6]

1. I see my body, dead for a few days, bloated, blue, festering.
2. I see my dead body infested with worms and flies.
3. I see that all that is left of my body is a skeleton with some flesh and blood still clinging to it.
4. I further consider my skeletal corpse without any flesh, yet still spotted with blood and held together with tendons.
5. All that is left of my dead body is a skeleton with no blood stains, held together by tendons.
6. I see that now all that is left is a collection of scattered bones. The bones of the feet have gone one way, the bones of the hand another. The thigh bones, pelvis, spinal vertebrae, jaw, teeth and skull have all come apart in different directions. They are all now just bare bones.
7. All that is left is a collection of bleached bones.

---

6. Adapted from U Silananda, *The Four Foundations of Mindfulness* (Boston: Wisdom Publications, 1990).

8. A year passes and I see that my dead body is reduced to being a pile of old bones.
9. These bones decay and become dust; blown apart and scattered by the wind, they cannot even be called bones anymore.

As with many deep truths, people tend to look at the death awareness meditations and say, Yes, I know all of that. I know I'm going to die someday. I know I can't take it with me. I know my body will be dust.

And as with other things – as with the law of impermanence itself – I would say we know it and we don't know it. We know it in our heads but haven't taken it into our hearts. We haven't let it penetrate the marrow of our bones. If we had, I can't help thinking we would live differently. Our whole lives would be different. The planet would be different as well.

If we really faced our fear of death – and these contemplations will bring it up, again and again – our lives would ultimately be lighter and more joyful. I don't propose death awareness to depress us. It enhances our ability to live more fully.

If we understood the reality of death, we would treat each other differently. Carlos Castaneda was once asked how we could make our lives more spiritual, and he said: Just remember that everyone you encounter today, everyone you see, will someday have to die. He's right. That knowledge changes our whole relationship to people.

During death awareness practice groups that I've led in Cambridge, I have asked people to leave the building after lunch, to walk around town, and to know that everyone they see will die; everyone is their brother or sister in death. It is a wonderful thing to do, especially after a period of death awareness meditation. It gives you a whole new attitude toward people you encounter.

Finally, life is a great teacher and death is a great teacher. Death is all around us, everywhere. For the most part – following the lead of our culture – we avoid it. But if we do open our hearts to this fact of our lives, it can be a great help to us. It can teach us how to live.

WHAT FOLLOWS

There is a certain irony to this chapter on death. On the one hand, it might be the most important subject in the book. It is what all the others have been leading up to and is in many ways the culmination of our practice. But we have no experience of it. We haven't died yet (that we know of).

We are aging all the time and can work with those teachings right away. We have all been sick, at least with minor illnesses, and will doubtless have another chance to work with illness soon. But in the case of death we have been talking only about reflections and visualizations. There will be only one time when we practice with dying. Only then will we see how we do.

There is a tradition in Buddhism, of course, of people actually sitting while they are dying. That is the way I would prefer to go out. But our preferences don't matter. We don't know what our circumstances will be when we die. We might be terribly feeble at the end of a debilitating illness, too weak to raise our heads, much less sit. We might be hit by a truck in the prime of life or have a heart attack. We might be surrounded by friends and family who support us in what we're going through. We might be utterly alone and in great pain. But no matter what our circumstances, we can practice with them. We can practice with anything. It is just a matter of remembering to do so.

And the strength of our practice in extraordinary moments – in even our last moments – will largely depend on how we have practiced up to then. If our mindfulness is strong, if it has become more natural to bring it to whatever is going on, the moment of death may be difficult but we will be able to practice with it.

Sometimes meditators engage in practices that seem extreme: sitting for hours without moving, sitting all night, sitting with great pain. Such practices help prepare us for serious illness or the time of death. If you get into the habit of practicing with difficult physical conditions, you are more likely to be ready for whatever comes up.

And I would like to emphasize that as extraordinary as the moment of death sounds, it will be just another moment. The same principles apply as always. Be with what is happening in your body and in your mind. Just be as you are. It should be a moment that you can approach in a fresh way. You will never have been through it before.

I believe that the key to experiencing that moment, and practicing with it, will be to come to it with what Suzuki Roshi called beginner's mind, what Zen Master Seung Sahn called don't-know mind, the mind that knows it doesn't know, that is willing to live in a place of not knowing. What gets in the way of that mind is expectations that people have about death and about what comes after. It is best to approach that moment – and every moment – with as few expectations as possible.

My fellow vipassana teacher Rodney Smith, who has done hospice work for many years, says that some of the most difficult deaths he has seen were of people who expected death to be a spiritual experience. That doesn't mean it won't be spiritual. It just means it is best to approach it without that expectation, without any expectation at all.

When I speak of beginner's mind or don't-know mind, I am not speaking of ignorance. I am speaking of knowing – being aware – that you don't know, an intentional turning against the mind's tendency to believe things, to think that it knows, to take comfort in accumulated knowledge. This is the openness and naïveté that is at the heart of dharma practice. It is both the end of a process and its beginning. It is the basis of really being alive.

I can make an analogy with another discipline. In Japan, when men were preparing to be samurai, they had to go through arduous training, analogous to that for a spiritual practice. They had to get their bodies into magnificent shape to be ready for combat. They had to learn all kinds of intricate maneuvers with swords and other weapons. They also had to train their minds to be ready for the psychological stress.

But when they had finally finished their training, when they had learned all the various strategies and were ready for combat at the highest level, they had to learn how to anticipate . . .

nothing. They had to go into combat expecting nothing. Perhaps with an inferior opponent, it might have worked to go in with a planned strategy, to anticipate what he might do. But at the highest level you had to leave your mind empty and clear, anticipating nothing, so you were ready for anything. You never knew what a truly great opponent might do. Buddhism sometimes speaks of this global awareness without attachment as seeing in ten directions, a kind of comprehensive alertness. You are just attentive.

But that didn't mean you could pull a guy off the street, ask him if he knew anything about combat, and if he said no, reply, "Great. That's don't-know mind," and throw him into combat. There is a great deal of technical skill that may lie behind not knowing. And that not knowing is a higher kind of wisdom. It is the organic intelligence that an empty, silent mind has.

One way to reach don't-know mind is to look at the mind that does know, or at least thinks it does, and understand how it learns things. We learn first of all from our families, our parents and siblings. Often family attitudes are very strong and offer a whole particular view of the world. Beyond knowledge that we gain from families is the knowledge of an ethnic group. There is also a kind of knowledge that has to do with our origins in a particular economic class. And there is the knowledge of being from a certain community and a certain country. You know your way around and know the customs of that place.

There is the knowledge that we get from books and classes, from study in general, and from working with a teacher. There is the kind of knowledge that comes from immersing our-selves in a particular discipline. And there is also, of course, street wisdom, the knowledge that we pick up simply by living out each day. I heard a great deal about that when I was younger, growing up in Brooklyn. "I may not have gone to college, but I've been to the school of life, and I've learned some things that all your fancy books can't teach." You've probably met some graduates from this school too.

Yet I'm sure you're also able to see, even as I enumerate them, the tremendous limitations of all these kinds of knowl-edge. We probably all had the experience, when we were young and seeing through the eyes of a child, of going to some other kid's house and discovering what a strange new world that was. If our friend was from a different ethnic background or social class, it was doubly strange. If he was from another country it was positively exotic.

One evening when I was teaching a class in Cambridge a couple of Mormon missionaries came to attend. Perhaps you've seen Mormon missionaries in your town too; they're quite distinctive, in white shirts, narrow ties, dark suits. They stood up during the question period and challenged me, chal-lenged Buddhism, saying that it didn't express a belief in God or acknowledge the supremacy of Christ. It was just an Asian psychology with nothing spiritual about it.

It really wasn't to the point to answer the questions they were bringing up. They were using the class as an occasion to proselytize. So I took another approach, trying to get them to see that all belief systems, all systems of knowledge, have inherent limitations, even though they claim to be universal.

"Listen," I said. "I know you think that your religion is true and mine is false. But you were born in Utah as Mormons, and I was born in Brooklyn as a Jew. Do you think that if our positions had been reversed, we'd be sitting here arguing the same sides?"

The missionary, alas, said that God had seen to it that he would have the good fortune to be born in Utah. But I think some other people saw my point.

All of knowledge has limitations, and they aren't just the limitations of being somehow provincial. The real limitation of knowledge – however broad – is that it has a way of interpreting our experience. It sees things through the eyes of yesterday. The thinking mind jumps in front of our experience and tells us what is happening – using past experience as a guide – then runs back into our mind and hides, so we have no idea that thinking ever came along. We believe we know what we just went through. But our beliefs may not be in accord with what actually happened.

That is why don't-know mind opens us up to a new kind of freedom. You learn through awareness practice to see how thought comes out of hiding and interprets your experience. You learn to recognize a thought, to see that a thought is just a thought; it isn't reality. You learn to let thoughts come and go without attaching to them. You then have a chance to see what your experience really is. The more you don't know, the more you see.

That is the positive side of don't-know mind. What if, for instance, you lived in Massachusetts but had heard that Rhode Island was an absolutely wonderful state, far superior? You would head in that direction. But there would finally come a moment when you would have to make a decision, to take it on faith. You would step out of Massachusetts and into Rhode Island.

The known and unknown are like that. The unknown contains a kind of deep stillness, a radiant purity of mind. But to get to that, you need to leave the known. You finally have to step out of the one and be in the other. Often fear of the unknown is just a reluctance to give up the known, because the known is the material out of which we create the self. It is familiar and gives us some sense of security, even if it isn't working very well.

Whatever your cultural or religious background, you have been taught something about death. (You may have been taught that it is a state of nothingness, of annihilation. You may believe that you "know" that.) It is not my intention to erase that teaching and substitute another. There are plenty of books that outline Buddhist beliefs on death, and you can find such knowledge in them.

But that is just one more belief system, one more kind of knowing. And I'm not sure that any system of knowing will be true to that final experience. When we enter the realm of death, we will abandon all forms of knowing. We will abandon everything. We won't be Buddhists, Christians, Jews. We won't have a family or ethnic group or country. We won't have a name. We'll be devoid of everything.

We need to acknowledge also that – despite all the teachings that reassure us – there is something deeply mysterious and poignant about death. I have lost both my parents in the past few years, and it was one thing to watch all the changes they went through as they approached death, quite another to take in the fact that they had died, that they were actually gone.

There is something similarly mysterious and wonderful about birth, about coming into this world. There is a way to go beyond birth and death, and this liberation is the goal of practice. But there is also something marvelous about life, which is wonderful when we have it, and which we in no way want to reject. Liberation does not ask us to reject it.

Dogen expressed it beautifully. "Everyday life is a noble life. The body that maintains this life is a noble body. Do not waste your life. Do not neglect your body. Respect the body, and adore this life."

The subject of death naturally brings up the question of what will happen afterward, and here I am afraid I will disappoint some readers. Students do come to me with questions about what happens after death. Often they are looking for a degree of certainty, some belief that will relieve them of the anxiety we all feel about this question. I am able to tell them what Buddhist teaching is. I can refer them to books – like *The Tibetan Book of the Dead* – that describe what supposedly happens in detail. But I can't tell them I know these things are true. I can't offer them certainty. I haven't died yet.

What I have always loved about Buddhism is that it isn't just a belief system, at least not in the forms I have taken up. It is a practice. There are teachings, but the Buddha always said not to believe them on his say-so. He said to try them out yourself and see if they prove to be true.

Death Is Unavoidable

He did leave various teachings on the subject of death. Some commentators have thought they were later teachings from someone other than the Buddha, but my best evaluation of the material is that the Buddha did have quite a bit to say on death. And because his teachings in so many other areas have proven themselves true in my practice, I'm inclined to believe these as well. But I don't *know* them to be true, as I know other things. There is a big difference between knowing and believing.

There are all kinds of beliefs about life after death. Buddhism, Hinduism, Islam, Christianity, Judaism, Native American religions, and any number of religions that we know less about, all have their beliefs. They all claim to reflect a revelation that someone had about this great mystery. They have some similarities and some differences. And of course some people, like the Marxists, insist with all the confidence of the truest believer that there is no life after death.

But beliefs – by definition – cannot be known. They can be strongly held; people have gotten into fights, even gone to war, over them. But beliefs are about the unknown, and the known, as I've said, cannot know the unknown. Often people are fearful about the unknown and establish some belief system to comfort themselves. The fierceness with which they hold the belief is a measure of their fear. But as long as they hold it, the fear will remain and will keep them from living the full life they are capable of.

I prefer to hold the belief in rebirth and the supposed comfort that comes along with it lightly, and to take up any fear that arises and deal with it directly, meeting the fear intimately as it expresses itself and lives out its life. It isn't that I haven't had intimations, some rather convincing, about what might follow death. I have. But I don't have certainties. I don't want to pretend to more than I have seen.

The image often used about rebirth is that life is the ocean and we are the waves. Our individual wave rises, builds, crests, breaks, and falls away – the wave ends – but it is still an expression of the ocean. It is a part of life. I, like others, have entered deep states of meditation and seen the profound undivided stillness that exists beneath the waves of life. I have also – like others – had visions of past lives while I meditated. (The Buddha, on the night when he achieved enlightenment, is supposed to have seen all his past lives.) But I don't know for certain that they were past lives. They may just have been visions.

I continue to maintain don't-know mind in the face of this mystery, but I am willing to believe there may be people who actually do know. When I began teaching death awareness and was confronted by this whole question, I got in touch with one of my teachers, Vimala Thakar, and told her of my dilemma: I wanted to pass on the Buddha's teachings about death but felt I didn't know them by my own experience, the way I have known other things I have taught. She made a striking response, in terms both of what I don't know and of what she does.

"Learning keeps the process of life fresh and green. Repeating the pregathered knowledge makes life stale and stinking. Congratulations for having the strength and urge to learn and live what you understand.

Death Is Unavoidable

"Rebirth is a fact. The ripples on the ocean of creative energy are called birth and death. At the deeper layer in the womb of the ocean there are neither ripples nor waves. A consciousness settled in the dimension of meditation is set free of the movement of birth and death. That is how I have seen the truth of birth and death as well as the mystery of deathless life."

I have had a glimpse of what Vimala points out, but I don't live there. There may be some people who know what I don't. I feel sure there are. But acknowledging the limits of what I know – and also not wanting to make my teaching "stale and stinking" – I would like briefly to review my understanding of the Buddha's teaching about rebirth.

We are entering the realm of our final two contemplations.

*I will grow different, separate from all that is dear
and appealing to me.*

*I am the owner of my actions, heir to my actions, born
of my actions, related through my actions, and live
dependent on my actions. Whatever I do, for good or
for ill, to that will I fall heir.*

I will primarily deal with these two contemplations in the next chapter, but they are also to the point here. The first four contemplations all seem to be bad news. We grow old, we get sick, we die, and we have to give up everything that is dear to us. It is only the fifth contemplation that leaves us any hope at all, though it is a somewhat mysterious statement, written in a culture where people believed in some doctrine of rebirth. It is a reference to the law of karma, stating that all we finally have, all we are heir to, is our actions. The law of karma brings along with it, in the minds of most people, the subject of rebirth.

We need to distinguish here between reincarnation, which is a Hindu doctrine, and rebirth, which is Buddhist. The doctrine of reincarnation states – to simplify somewhat – that we have an eternal soul that migrates from body to body purifying itself through successive lives until it achieves a final perfection and unites with God.

The doctrine of rebirth is somewhat different. The Buddha taught that there is no part of us as individuals that is eternal and unchanging; everything is a process of change. At the time of death that process continues. The body decays and becomes something else (as is detailed in the charnel ground meditations), but there is a mental continuum that goes on as well and also keeps changing. When conditions are right it takes on a new body. Everything is a matter of the conditions coming together; it is codependent arising. One of the conditions is this mental continuum, and when the other conditions join it, a new being is created.

The image that is sometimes used is of one candle being lighted from another. Imagine you have a candle that is burned all the way down, to the point that it is barely lit. Just as it is about to go out, you light another candle from it, and suddenly the flame burns brighter. Is that the same flame, or is it different? It doesn't seem quite right to say either thing.

The doctrine of rebirth is like that. It isn't that there is a single soul, a single entity, migrating from body to body. There is a constant process of change, and a continuum between the two bodies.

Once upon a time you were an embryo in the womb. Then you were a newborn babe. Now, perhaps, you are a middle-aged woman. Is that woman the same as the baby? Is she different? It seems wrong to say either thing. (And yet, what happened to the baby? It's gone, but it didn't die.) Rebirth is like that. The mental continuum goes on, and when conditions are right, it takes shape in a new body.

Sometimes students say, "I believe in a soul. Doesn't Buddhism allow for belief in a soul?" That depends. If I go down deep, I do find a certain psychic aggregate, with a characteristic suchness, that is Larry Rosenberg–ness. But it isn't an unchanging entity. It too – like everything else – is a process. So if you are asking if there is anything like a soul right now, Buddhism might say yes, there is a relative pattern to the process that is going on. But if you are asking if it is unchanging and eternal, Buddhism would say no.

This doctrine of rebirth makes perfect sense to me. It is consistent with everything else that the Buddha taught, and I have found many of those teachings to be true. But do I *know* the doctrine of rebirth to be true? I don't. It just seems quite plausible.

What creates this mental continuum – as the fifth contemplation states – is our actions. That is the law of karma. All our actions have some result. Our present experience has a connection to actions and thoughts from the past, and what we think and do now will have results in the future.

Again, I don't know the exact way in which the law of karma has consequences from one rebirth to another. But I am definitely convinced it applies to this lifetime. Our thoughts and actions have vast importance and far-reaching consequences right here and right now.

It is for that reason that I don't spend a great deal of time worrying about the doctrine of rebirth. A wrong action may or may not cause suffering in a future lifetime, but it definitely causes suffering in this one. We suffer in the act of doing it or very soon thereafter. Similarly, kind and generous actions are beneficial to ourselves and to others in our life right now. So I don't need the motivation of a future life. There is plenty of motivation right now. Of course, if the consequences of avoiding harmful actions and cultivating beneficial ones extend into future lifetimes, it will be a great bonus. We have everything to gain and nothing to lose.

In the same way, the path of awareness that I have chosen seems to me the right path whether it leads to a better rebirth or not. Buddhist teachings talk about rebirth in great detail. They say, for instance, that the condition of your mind at the time of death has much to do with the quality of your next rebirth. Most beneficial is a mind that is aware and equanimous. That may be true. But even if it isn't, I would like to be aware at the moment of death, just because I know from experience that aware is the best way to be.

I would go even further. Suppose someone could prove to me that all of Buddhism is a sham. The Buddha never lived; his teachings were all made up years after his supposed life; there is no such thing as enlightenment; and there is definitely no rebirth. I would still live the way I do. What would be better, not to be aware? To have a mind that is scattered and unreliable? Not to take care with my thoughts and actions? To lie, cheat, steal, and count on the insatiable nature of craving for happiness? I live the way I do not because of my belief in some doctrine but because it is the best way to live that I have found.

It would be good to have a favorable rebirth but better still to go beyond birth and death altogether. The real goal of our practice is not better and better rebirths – which may happen in the future – but liberation, which happens in the present. The rebirths I am certain of are those that take place moment by moment, as we constantly create new selves. Real liberation is to see that process but not be caught up in it, to be free of it.

It is time, then, to turn our attention to the process of liberation and to the last of the messengers that the Buddha encountered, the wandering monk. We have given our full attention to the process of birth and death. Now we must discover how to be free of it.

THE FOURTH MESSENGER
Heirs to Our Actions

No one can die fearlessly and in complete security until they have truly realized the nature of mind, for only this realization, deepened over years of sustained practice, can keep the mind stable during the molten chaos of the process of dying.

—SOGYAL RINPOCHE

DIE NOW

AFTER THE Buddha, as a young prince, had learned the reality of aging, sickness, and death, he encountered a fourth messenger, a wandering contemplative. This man had no home. He had no family. He had no loved ones; that is, he treated everyone with love and showed no favoritism to anyone. When the prince questioned him, he stated quite specifically that he had adopted this way of life because he was terrified of birth and death. He was searching for that blessed state in which destruction is not known. Meeting him, the prince knew that he wanted to make a similar choice.

This person had chosen the path of a contemplative, facing

up to the ultimate fact of death, which is well stated by our fourth contemplation: "I will grow different, separate from all that is dear and appealing to me." The contemplative brings about these separations sooner rather than later. He gives up most of the things that the rest of us are attached to.

This is still the strategy that Theravada monastics use today. They know they are going to have to give up everything eventually, so they give up nearly everything now. They leave their homes and families, own only robes and a bowl, and are dependent on the generosity of laypeople. They eat one meal a day, don't handle money, and are celibate.

I have great respect for the monastic life, though I have not chosen to live it myself. It is one proven strategy to maximize the possibility of getting free. The fourth messenger had achieved some measure of liberation and was living in a manner designed to bring complete inner freedom.

But becoming a monastic or a wanderer does not in itself make one free. The Buddha didn't find freedom just because he became a wanderer. It took him six years, and he made some false starts. So just being a monk isn't enough. It is possible to be attached to a robe and a bowl. And it is definitely possible to be attached to one's identity as a monk, to one's opinions and views, to have pride in the advanced level of one's dharma practice.

When I was in Korea, for instance, practicing for a year in various Zen temples, I had a beautiful robe, which someone in Seoul had sewn for me. When I was leaving, one of the monks asked if we could swap robes. He was hesitant, but he did approach me. He figured I was a layperson and the robe wasn't really important to me, and he really wanted to have mine.

I also knew a monk in Thailand, a Canadian, who admitted to me that he was frequently obsessed with the idea that he was a monk. There were times when it was all he could think about.

In contrast to that, J. Krishnamurti was known for wearing fine clothes and driving a Mercedes. But whatever country he was in, he adopted the customs of that place. In India he dressed quite differently than in this country. And when people admired some item of his clothing, he would offer to give it to them, and often did. He had and enjoyed beautiful things but didn't seem attached to them at all.

The monastic attempts to free himself by having few possessions and letting go of his attachment to persons and things. But the Buddha made it quite clear that his teachings are for all of us, and we as laypeople need a different approach to accomplish the same ends. Our lives generally include family, sexual relationships, the need to work to earn money, and eating more than one meal per day. We use the practice to learn to live skillfully in these areas. When we do, our lives become more harmonious, and these areas themselves provide us with fertile materials for practice.

The Buddha told us that we suffer because we cling to things in a world of change. The way to end our suffering is to cease clinging. If we could really give up our attachments and die to things now, we would no longer fear death, because we would have nothing to lose. We would already have given everything up.

We don't have to wait for death to realize the benefits of giving up our attachments. Such letting go is one of the most creative acts a human being can perform and brings with it a whole new energy. That energy isn't something we cultivate, and it doesn't become one of our acquisitions. It simply emerges as we give up our attachments. It flowers as our attachments wither.

Abandoning our attachments can sound like a depressing task. The very thought may bring up feelings of sadness and vulnerability, as the ego is being deprived of a primary source of nourishment. But this letting go brings with it clarity and brightness. It opens up to a dimension of incomparable fulfillment, peace, and joy.

That is an easy thing to say, of course, but not so easy to do. Giving up attachments is not something we do once and for all, then are done. It is an ongoing process, all our lives. But I want to emphasize that it is also not something to think of as being far off in the future, the way we sometimes think we will practice for years and finally achieve something called awakening. Liberation – like death – is not a goal that sits at the end of a long road. It happens now, and only now. It is present this moment if we want to choose it.

I said in the last chapter that I don't know if karma operates from one rebirth to another, but I am absolutely certain it operates in this lifetime: We commit some action and it has a result. In the same way, there are births and deaths that take place in this life, moment by moment. We are constantly giving birth to new selves. There is definitely a way to be free of that world of birth and death. And that freedom is to be found only in the moment. The teachings on karma are not just a belief system. They are a way to approach the present moment, to take better care of your life by taking care of your mind.

The present moment is shaped by present actions and previous ones, the results of present and past intentions. Sometimes the consequences of past actions are so strong that all you can do is hold your ground with as much awareness as possible and weather the storm until it passes. But when the power of past action is not so great, there is room to intervene with awareness and direct our energy in a more beneficial way. It is possible to make good karma.

It is in this sense that our fifth reflection provides us with a ray of hope in the face of the others. The first four remind us that we are subject to aging, sickness, and death and must finally separate from all that is dear to us. These are facts of existence that are out of our control. The fifth reflection ("I am the owner of my actions, heir to my actions, born of my actions, related through my actions, and live dependent on my actions. Whatever I do, for good or for ill, to that will I fall heir") points out what is in our control: our thoughts and our intentions. When we approach any condition of the body with the intention to see clearly and understand, rather than to judge, we change the experience of that moment.

Karma is essentially intention, the energy that directs human action. Going along with the strongly conditioned habit of grasping or aversion is its own karma, a mind-state that feels constricted, narrow, and cloudy. The choice to observe rather than react, on the other hand, brings immediate results, a more open, clear, and spacious state of mind.

Every moment of intention is a moment of karma, and whenever there is karma there is an immediate result. Even a small thought averse to signs of our aging is not empty of consequences. When such moments accumulate they bring with them a great deal of unnecessary suffering, and through repetition and increased intensity they can expand into character traits. They give rise to a story of an elderly "me" saturated with self-pity.

If instead of such identification we intervene with mindfulness and equanimity, we short-circuit this process and prevent unnecessary suffering. We take better care of the immediate present and prevent such unskillful moments from oppressing us in the future. In this moment we can heal past wounds, shape the quality of the present, and plant seeds that are beneficial for the future.

Some people mistakenly view the Buddha's teaching on karma as fatalistic. It is not at all. We are not helpless, because our situation is workable, and it is workable because it is observable. The body may be old, sick, and wrinkled, but it is possible for a mind established in meditation to be young, fresh, sensitive, and clear to the very end. As Soen Roshi said, practice "turns your miserable karma into your wonderful dharma."

This is what Buddhist teachers mean when they speak of the great death, and we can come to it at any time. It is what Krishnamurti was pointing toward when he said we must die day to day, moment to moment. It is the death of the ego. Once this death has taken place, there is none other to worry about. There is nothing but the body that is left to die.

Let me try to explain more concretely. Moment by moment we create many selves, largely by thinking. Sometimes they may involve major things: I am the Larry Rosenberg who just led a wonderful retreat, or taught a great class, or published a book. Sometimes they are smaller things: I am the Larry Rosenberg who is kind to waitresses, or thoughtful to his wife, or helpful around the house.

There is no problem with these things in themselves. (And they are not always good things. Sometimes I am the Larry Rosenberg who led a retreat that didn't seem to work out or who taught a class unskillfully.) The problem is that we make self out of them: I am Larry Rosenberg, Leader of Retreats, Teacher of Classes. We carry that load of ego around with us. We often create a massive persona out of the succession of small happenings that make up our experience. But it is all extra: It is a creation of our minds. We have created out of thinking a sense of self that doesn't exist in any solid enduring way.

When we practice sitting meditation, we see ourselves engaging in this process again and again. If nothing else, we think what good or bad meditators we are. But that isn't the only time we do it. We engage in it constantly. If we take our awareness practice away from our cushions and into our everyday lives, we see ourselves doing it all day long.

The law of karma comes into this kind of birth and death as well. Of course it is an expression of wisdom to create good karma: to be loving to your wife, kind to a waitress, helpful as a teacher. These actions yield beneficial results. Try them out. It is harmful to create bad karma, to scream at people in traffic, snap at a clerk who gives you the wrong change. But it is better yet when you create no karma, when there is no one there to take credit or blame. Things just happen, and there is no attachment to them whatsoever.

It is similar to what I say to students about self-esteem. Certainly it is better to have good self-esteem than bad self-esteem. It would be a terrible thing to walk around all the time thinking (for instance): I'm a terrible teacher; nobody learns anything in my classes; nobody profits from my retreats. But what people find hard to understand is that good self-esteem is a similarly heavy burden. For one thing, maintaining it is a full-time occupation. You have to be on guard constantly. It is also just a big load to be carrying around. It is unnecessary.

In the Zen tradition, there are the famous words of Lin Chi, who spoke of the true person of no rank. Such a person doesn't feel superior to other people. He doesn't feel inferior to them. And he doesn't feel the same. The whole process of comparison doesn't enter his mind. He has stepped out of the status game altogether.

The true person of no rank has died the great death. He has no other death to fear.

So the problem with our attachments is not really the things themselves, the objects, the people, the achievements. The problem is that we make self out of them. I am the owner of a Lexus. The president of a company. The father of three fine children. We create a self out of these things, and we believe that is who we are. And when we think of dying, we imagine losing these things, and we're terrified. But what we're most afraid of losing is the sense of self.

The question is: Can we lose it now? Can we start to die each day, each moment?

The process of giving up attachments – or at least noticing them – happens naturally as we age. We try to maintain various images of ourselves, and these images have a head-on collision with reality. We get a very good look at them. We see that we've been building a self out of a set of conditions. But as you age you see clearly that these things are not solid and that they never were. I don't mean to imply that this is an easy process. There can be some real grieving involved as cherished self-images break into pieces. But it is also an opportunity to get free of them and enter into a more fulfilling dimension of consciousness.

The practice of not-selfing – not creating a self out of attachments – is a simple but subtle one. It isn't necessary to reject the selves that we create. Actually, pushing them away is just another form of clinging. All we have to do is clearly see that act of creating self. It is a simple matter of awareness. In that moment of seeing, and silent understanding, the self falls away. It can't withstand the bright light of clear awareness. Then, in the next moment, a new self can be created. So the practice of not-selfing requires constant vigilance. And it always takes place in the present.

That isn't to say that there aren't larger experiences. It does seem that sometimes large chunks of self just fall away. We see clearly that there is no solid self and feel a new sense of freedom. Perhaps we are then less likely to create self too. But selfing happens in subtle ways, and very rapidly.

Emptiness of self, for instance, can itself become an attachment, as in the famous exchange between the great Chinese master Chao Chou and Venerable Yen Yang.

"When not a single thing is brought," Yen Yang asks, "then what?"

"Put it down," Chao Chou replies.

"If I don't bring a single thing," Yen Yang asks, "what should I put down?"

"Then carry it out," Chao Chou says.[1]

It is possible to achieve emptiness by giving up all our obvious attachments, then keep the process of selfing alive through a subtle idea of accomplishment: "I don't mind aging and have no fear of death." We must look carefully to see if such utterances are authentic or the voice of highly refined delusion. The ego is brilliant; we cut off one head and another springs up. We need to see that even emptiness is empty.

To give a small example from my own life: When I first started practicing vipassana, I would describe it to my friends with considerable excitement. Some of them, despite all I said, seemed unimpressed, and I would be hurt and get defensive. After all, I had found a practice that seemed right for me and had made many sacrifices for it. But at this point in my life, I rarely think about how someone else feels about it. I don't identify the path with a self. To really practice vipassana meditation, you have to give up being a vipassana meditator.

---

1. Thomas Cleary, trans., *The Book of Serenity* (Hudson, N.Y.: Lindisfarne Press, 1990), Case 57: "Yan Yang's Thing."

The freedom that I'm talking about involves the dissolution of all the psychological enclosures that we construct to protect ourselves, everything that we think of as our identity. There is fear connected with this freedom, really the same as the fear of death: we're afraid of losing who we think we are. But we can work with that fear, which arises and passes away, and see that it too is an impermanent phenomenon. Through that process of insightful knowing, we gradually dissolve the sense of self. We practice dying on the installment plan.

As we mentioned before, many people can go along with this idea when it has to do with concepts or personal possessions. But they balk when it comes to people. It seems to them natural, for instance, to be attached to their children. It is just a matter of loving them very much. But love is not the same thing as attachment. Love does not imply the creation of a self and the possessiveness that frequently accompanies it. As a matter of fact, we can really love only when we drop the self. Attachment implies a holding on, wanting things to be a certain way, setting conditions. But real love is unconditional. It is unattached to any outcome.

When you give up attachments, you are not rejecting the people who are closest to you. You are just relating to them in a radically new way.

What I'm describing here is not really anything new. We can call it the great death, but it is really just the natural outcome of the sustained daily practice of mindfulness.

Awareness practice is like that. It starts out sounding simple, disarmingly simple, and in a sense that never changes. What you tell meditation students after twenty minutes isn't that much different from what you tell them after twenty years. But as you do this practice over time, it progressively deepens, until finally you see that it is as large and mysterious as life itself. You gradually see all your addictions and attachments, until finally you come to the supreme addiction, the addiction to self. When you work with that one, you're working with all of them. You're also practicing death awareness, because it is the notion of a self that dies. There is nothing else to die.

You clearly see that you have been carrying a heavy burden. That seeing is a cleansing of consciousness. It is also a realization of the deepest teaching and a vast expansion of who we are. The best self-image in the world compared with the vast and silent nature of the mind itself is like a candle compared with sunlight.

It is a wonderful feeling to cleanse our consciousness in that way, to voluntarily give up our clinging and attachments. It is a prefiguring of death, but it turns out to be a huge relief. You're dying to a way of relating to things that was a major obstacle to dharma practice and to real living.

So our practice is about death, about coming fully to face death, but it is also about life, about learning how to live. It shines the light of death on life. If the Buddha had tried to practice in the palace, without facing the reality of aging, sickness, and death, his practice might have lacked urgency. We want to know if there is life after death, and that is certainly a valid concern. But the real question is whether there is life before death. Are we living now? It is only once we live with the awareness of death that we truly are.

BE THE KNOWING

The practice of liberation that I'm talking about, of dying every day, dying every moment, is intimately linked with don't-know mind. We begin our practice thinking we know who we are. *My name is So-and-so. I was born in this place. My parents were these people. I live here. My characteristics are as follows.* But the more we practice, the more we see through these stories of me and my life. Finally we get to a place where there is nothing left. No identification remains. We don't know who we are. But we *really* don't know. And we are not waiting any longer for a conceptual answer, because such not knowing is true knowing. Our essence is not a notion or a representation of any kind. It just is.

It is like the famous story of Bodhidharma and the emperor Wu in China. The emperor was an active patron of Buddhism and believed that he knew a great deal, but in encountering Bodhidharma he was meeting someone who had gone very deeply into meditation. He asked a couple of questions about doctrine and didn't get anything like the answers he was expecting. Finally, in exasperation, he said, "Who is it that is standing before me and giving me these answers?" And Bodhidharma said, "I have no idea." That answer did not express ignorance. It expressed the inadequacy of any notion in representing our true nature. It was a deep penetration of don't-know mind.

There is an analogous process that happens in sitting practice. When we begin, and being in the present moment is new to us, we tend to stay quite close to the breathing. In time the mind becomes reasonably stable, and we may open the practice to choiceless awareness, so we just watch everything, the breath, sensations in the body, mind-states. We have no agenda for what should turn up, and we make no choice for or against whatever does. We observe something simply because it is there. We see it all come, and we see it all go.

At first the feeling is that we're *doing* something, watching the breathing or the other objects, but in time that doing begins to fall away and what emerges is the effortless art of awareness, letting everything come and go. Still, the emphasis is somewhat on the objects. We feel the in-breath and out-breath, hear cars passing by, feel a twinge of pain in one knee, watch a wave of fear or panic arise. We can't help noticing that all these things are impermanent, that they arise and pass away.

Even that may not be true choiceless awareness. There is still some sense of observing and an observer; a subtle self-consciousness remains. There is a person sitting there doing choiceless awareness. But as we continue to sit over a period of months and years, the emphasis shifts. We don't bring the shift about. We can't bring it about. It just happens. That sense of deliberately observing, of being a meditator, withers away, sometimes just for periods of time, then for longer and longer. There is no longer an observer and an observed. There is no separation whatsoever.

What has happened is that the ego we've been talking about – the one who watches and identifies – has started to wither away. There is just sitting, pure awareness, with no effort whatsoever, an open, undivided connection with life as it is in this moment. It's as if all the things we were watching were the clouds in the sky, and now the blue sky itself begins to emerge. It isn't that the sky developed. It was there all along. We realize that it always has been. It was just obscured by the clouds.

That is what the forest masters mean when they tell us to be the knowing. But we don't have to try to be it. It's what we are. It is what we have been all along. There is nothing we do to get there. It just happens. As we continue to practice, we just keep getting deeper and deeper. As our sky nature becomes more obvious and stable, we experience the clouds in a more spacious context, and they cease to be problems.

It is because I have had a small taste of that state that I have some confidence in the Buddhist teachings on death. It is also because I've tasted of it that I am comfortable in a state of not knowing, because that deep serene place is not really one of knowing as we think of it but of not-knowing, of pure awareness. (Be the not-knowing, the forest masters might say.)

It is in that context that I would like to quote the words of the teacher who helped me so much in Thailand, Ajaan Maha Boowa. These remarks come from a talk he gave to a woman who was dying of cancer. She had come to the monastery to meditate while she was dying, and he spoke to her every evening.

On one occasion, he said:

> Even at the moment when you're about to die, the heart ... won't be shaken by pain and death, because it is sure that the mind is the mind, a stronghold of awareness....

The mind thus doesn't fear death because it is sure of itself, that it won't get destroyed anywhere. Discernment will spread its power far and wide. The heart will be more and more radiant, more and more courageous, because discernment is what cleanses it. Even if death comes at that moment, there is no problem. The pain will disappear, but the mind won't disappear. It will return to its mindness. If you use mindfulness and discernment to investigate pain without retreating, to the point where you understand it, then even when you are about to die, you will know that the pain will disappear first. The mind won't disappear. . . . The mind will withdraw itself from all that and revert to its mindness.[2]

And on another evening:

There is no need to fear death. . . . Don't create snares to catch yourself and hurt yourself. There is no death to the mind. There is nothing but awareness pure and simple. Death doesn't exist in the mind, which is something 100 percent unalterable and sure. . . . We human beings, when we have stopped breathing, are called dead people. At that moment, the knower separates from the elements, so that nothing is left but physical elements with no feelings. That's a dead person. But actually the knower doesn't die.[3]

---

2. Ajaan Maha Boowa, *Straight from the Heart* (Udorn Thani, Thailand: Wat Pa Baan Taad, 1998).
3. Ibid

Another teacher who speaks with the same confidence is the Korean master Ven. Song Chol, who emphasizes trusting in don't-know mind.

> We all possess pure, brilliant, expansive Fundamental Mind which remains unchanged throughout eternity. Its brilliance could not be matched by even a thousand suns rising together.
>
> To compare the huge, endless universe to this Fundamental Mind would be like comparing a single grain of millet to an endless ocean. This Fundamental Mind is unimaginable and indescribable, and to possess it is the greatest of all possible glories. This Mind is filled with complete wisdom and virtue, and is therefore called Natural Wisdom.
>
> This Natural Wisdom possessed by each of us is an inexhaustible treasure-house. And once the door to this treasure-house is opened, it reveals the greatest wisdom and virtue and the ultimate in human dignity.
>
> But people are unfamiliar with this treasure-house, and they search for Truth in such ancient dregs as the written and the spoken word, a quest that is as useless as searching for fire in ice.
>
> This Fundamental Mind can be compared to a mirror, and whether covered with dust or not, a mirror is a mirror. It remains unchanged no matter how long it is dirtied and covered with dust, and once the dust is removed, it gleams as brilliantly as ever.

Even gold dust is only dust to a mirror and an obstruction to its function. In the same way, words of the sages that appear to be golden jade are but dust on our Fundamental Mind and they merely darken it.

To see this clean, bright Fundamental Mind, you must wipe away the sages and wipe away the devils. Because the words of absolute religious leaders are great obstructions to and unhealthy influences on Fundamental Mind, those who believe in Buddha must rid themselves of Buddha and those who believe in Jesus must rid themselves of Jesus.

If we rid ourselves of Buddha and Confucius and Lao Tzu and Jesus, and all sages and devils, our minds become as clear as the blue skies; yet we have to destroy the blue sky as well if we are to discover our Fundamental Mind. There's no greater impediment to finding this Mind than fixating on the sages of the past and being unable to cast them aside.

In order to find true wisdom and eternal freedom and to see this Fundamental Mind, you must throw out these influences like you'd cast away poison. You have to treat Buddha and Jesus and Confucius and Lao Tzu as enemies, and rid yourself of them. They are but dust to Fundamental Mind and only make this Mind darker and darker. Wipe away the dust called Buddha and Jesus so that you may see this astounding Fundamental Mind.

Who are Buddha and Jesus? As I sit alone, forgetting saints and devils, the moon is more brilliant than ever as

it rises over mountains, and the fragrance of chrysanthe-
mums is incomparable.[4]

I have no idea how you will feel as you read these words.
Some readers may feel inspired, touched by great hope. Others may be skeptical. But this unshakable quality of mind is
the direction the practice is heading, whether you know it or
not. Every time you are mindful of a breath or of a morsel of
food, every time you take a mindful step, you are moving toward the radiant mind.

I don't know what will happen at the moment of my death,
but I do know that I want to be there for whatever it is, not in a
terrified way, with my thoughts all over the place, but with a
steady mind that has been trained by practice.

Some years ago I was talking to Tara Tulku Rinpoche about
my practice. I had a great deal of respect for him and wondered how he thought I was doing. Probably I was fishing for
compliments. He listened to things I said and responded to
them in different ways. Finally he ended our exchange. "Listen. Let me put it this way. Do you have absolute confidence in
your total indestructibility?"

What a question! I couldn't say that I did.

His implication was clear: Then keep practicing.

And that is the advice I would give to anyone who yearns to
feel that confidence.

---

4. Personal communication, translated from Korean.

THE PRACTICE
Intimacy with Living and Dying

THE SUBJECT of this book is intricately tied up with the practice we are using to examine it. If we could really grasp what the Buddha taught, we would have no problem with aging and death. If we could deeply see the truth of aging and death, we would understand what the Buddha taught. These facts of our lives are not problems to be solved or eliminated. They are ways of learning the deepest truths we can know. They are doorways to liberation.

Correct meditation practice is to learn to bring the same kind of attention to the rest of our lives that we give to moments on the cushion. The mindfulness that we develop as we sit expands until it fills the whole day. One of my favorite metaphors for mindfulness practice, one that has been extremely helpful to me, is to see it as the practice of intimacy.

The great thirteenth-century Zen master Eihei Dogen was once asked, What is the awakened mind? And he replied: The mind that is intimate with all things. The more we ponder that statement, the deeper it grows. The practice of intimacy ranges from the simple act of breathing all the way to the ultimate human experience, awakening, or liberation. It also covers everything in between.

The term *intimacy,* of course, is popular in our culture. We all want intimacy, or at least think we do, but what we actually feel is loneliness, separation, and isolation. And the fact is – though no one wants to hear this – that we can't have intimacy with another person until we're intimate with our loneliness. We can't be intimate with someone else until we're intimate with ourselves.

The larger subjects of this book – sickness, aging, and death – are extremely intimate. How could anything be closer to us? But we have a remarkable capacity to run away from them. We are running away from that which is closest to us. We can't really do that, of course. The basic facts of our lives are always right here. But we keep trying to do it, and thereby become intimate strangers with ourselves.

In one of his movies, Woody Allen says something like, "It's not that I'm afraid of dying, I just don't want to be there when it happens." We as practitioners are just the opposite. We are learning how to acknowledge openly our fear of dying. We even invite it to appear. And we most certainly do want to be there when death happens. We want to be there when everything happens, but certainly death. It can be a crucial test of a lifetime's devotion to the Buddha's path of awakening. We want to be intimate with those final moments.

Intimacy is an experience of nonseparation, of being at one with whatever is happening. We tend to think that we are not all right now – we're too fearful, greedy, angry, whatever – but that if we take up some spiritual practice we can improve ourselves. We will be all right at some moment in the future.

We have "in order to" mind; we are always doing *this* in order to get *that,* or in order to *be* that. Yet that very tendency – to strive, be ambitious, be preoccupied with a goal, get ahead of ourselves – takes us out of the present moment, away from how we are now. It can actually prevent intimacy. Then we complain that we don't have it. Our wish for intimacy can prevent us from being intimate.

One of my favorite Buddhist traditions is the Soto Zen lineage of Kosho Uchiyama, which has been brought to this country by Shohaku Okumura and a number of other people who have translated Uchiyama's work. Uchiyama himself was the disciple of an earlier teacher, Sawaki Roshi, and their exchanges inform several of Uchiyama's books.

Sawaki, who had a difficult, orphaned childhood, and who rocked the Japanese Zen establishment by taking over a ruined temple and practicing a very austere form of Zen, was apparently a powerful and charismatic teacher, while Uchiyama presents himself in his writing as being timid and weak. At one point he says to Sawaki, "If I practice *zazen* [meditation] for many years, will I be as strong as you?"

Sawaki, without a moment's hesitation, says, "No. You won't. I've always been this way. *Zazen* didn't do this for me."

He said he wanted his epitaph to read, "Here lies Sawaki Roshi. Wasted his whole life sitting on a cushion." He was famous for saying that *zazen* was entirely useless. (But if you don't wholeheartedly do this useless activity, he would say, your whole life will be useless.) He was trying to counteract "in order to" mind and insisted that his students sit just to sit.

On the one hand, sitting is one of the most practical things you can do. It definitely has beneficial effects on your life, as anyone will tell you who does it. But when you sit in order to gain them – the way Uchiyama wanted to be like Sawaki – you undermine yourself. You limit what sitting can do. It is fine to have a sincere aspiration to be a free and sane person; that can give enthusiasm and direction to your practice. But very often we put something in front of us to run after, and that separates us from full and direct contact with the present moment. A corner of the mind is occupied with the goal and is unable to see what is right now.

One of the major ways I teach is by leading nine-day silent retreats, often at the Insight Meditation Society in Barre, Massachusetts. There is no question in my mind that these retreats are beneficial and that they are a wonderful way to deepen one's practice. To the people who do them, they represent a substantial investment of time and energy. Some people come from far away, and most have taken time off from work and separated from their families. They have often been looking forward to the retreat for months.

So it is natural for them to arrive at the retreat with some idea of how they want it to be or what they want to get from it. Often they want to reduce the stress in their lives or find some peace. They might want to work out a particular problem, take a hard look at a relationship. They may want to access their creativity or have some important insights. Vipassana meditation is also known as insight meditation, and people who come on retreat want to have some of these insights. They don't know what they are, but they want them.

But comically, and characteristically, they find that quite the opposite happens. Being on retreat itself can be rather stressful, at least at first; you're in a new place and your old routines have been taken away from you – reading, writing, even talking – and you have been assigned a new and sometimes uninviting or difficult job for the work period. Your mind might respond to the silence by doing a lot of internal chatter, and you also may find yourself having relationship problems on retreat, with your roommate or your work partner or those annoying people who take so long in the lunch line. Your mind isn't having any insights; it's the same old mind you had at home. You might as well be there. You begin to wish you were.

The whole problem is your expectations, your hidden agenda about how the retreat was supposed to be, because those notions take you out of the present moment. Life just keeps being how it is, no matter what we hope for or expect. There is a gap between the way things are and the way we want them to be, and that gap is filled with suffering. Such suffering doesn't happen just on retreat. It happens every day of our lives. Practice involves a profound form of reeducation, taking our mind away from what we want to happen and planting it in the middle of what really is happening.

Ultimately – though we use them as skillful means and they are useful methods – the essence of practice is not about sitting or walking meditation. Practice is about being with the experience of the present moment. Right now. However it is.

Awareness with equanimity is the key – attention not distorted by grasping or pushing away.

Often I have students – especially new students – who come to me and say they've just had a really good sitting. It was exactly the way they thought it should be. They finally know what meditation is all about. And I think, Too bad. If you've just had a good sitting, a bad sitting can't be far behind, because you'll show up expecting the same thing again. The same thing never happens again. We have a mathematical equation in dharma circles: Expectation equals suffering.

The practice of intimacy, on the other hand, is just being with the experience as it is. People are assigned jobs on retreats – vacuuming the floor, for instance – and wonder how they can be intimate with that. They often try to strong-arm their way into it, to bring some kind of extraordinary attention to what they're doing. That lasts about twenty seconds. A better way is to give yourself to the vacuuming in a relaxed way and just watch what happens. See how thoughts come up, of working more quickly so you can take a walk, perhaps. They separate you from what you're doing. Don't fight the process; just – in that act of seeing – come back to the task. There will then be moments, which will gradually increase, when you are with it completely. Intimacy comes from the clear seeing of separation.

You have probably had the experience of intimacy I'm talking about without necessarily calling it that. It is that moment when the subject/object dichotomy dissolves, when there is no longer a person performing an activity; there is just the activity. Musicians have told me that they sometimes get so absorbed in their instrument that playing it becomes that way, absolutely effortless.

Athletes are famous for getting into a zone, but sometimes perfectly ordinary people do the same thing, when they get so involved in an activity like running or swimming that the doer just disappears. Good dancers often do, too, either with a partner or by themselves; suddenly there are no people present, there is just dancing. One thought can spoil the whole thing. You think, "I'm at one with dancing," and your self-consciousness returns.

These moments happen because we are devoted to the activity and give ourselves to it fully. The aim of practice is to give yourself to everything that way, not in the hope of some reward, but just because it is your life at that moment. The fulfillment is in the doing. We use the simple act of sitting as a way of practicing that kind of abandon.

At first when we sit we are like a child learning to ride a bicycle; we are conscious of our body and breathing and feel a certain awkwardness and self-consciousness in the whole situation. But after a while riding a bike becomes second nature – it's as if the child and the bicycle have become one – and sitting is the same way. The mind, body, and breathing merge. It's as if you're not breathing but being breathed. You can't find a breather anywhere.

One metaphor for this experience of intimacy is rawness, like raw food. Our moment-by-moment experience simply *is* a certain way. We say we have a pain in the back, but really that feeling is completely unique and constantly changing. Even the word *pain* isn't true to it, just an approximation, and already an interpretation, a negative one at that. There is just a feeling, entirely unique and in perpetual flux; there is a flow of feeling. That is what we sense as we get very still on our meditation cushion – the constantly flowing energy of life.

What we do with this raw experience is to cook it, with concepts, theories, explanations, descriptions. Soon it becomes an idea in our heads, quite far from the original experience. We lose the *is*ness of it.

Mindfulness is the practice of coming back to that *is*ness, that flow of experience, raw and wild, direct and naked. Being intimate with it.

One example I often use to help people understand intimacy is watching sports on television. You may love basketball and know everything about it, but when you turn on the television you are also listening to a commentator, who tells you what is happening as if you can't see it for yourself and who actually changes the experience. Commentators are paid to make the game exciting or to support one team or another. Our minds are commentators, too, with hidden agendas all their own. We may not be able to turn that commentator off, or even turn it down, but we can see it for what it is, the way our mind cooks everything that happens. In that seeing we come back to our raw experience.

WATCHING YOUR ESCAPES

What, for instance, is intimacy with reading this book? First, you know that you're sitting; you feel the contact of your body with the chair and of your feet with the floor. You notice the breathing. That is good grounding for any act of mindfulness, to get in touch with your physical posture and your breathing.

Then – as they say in the Zen tradition – you just read. Your eyes move across the page; you see the words and absorb them, taking in their meaning. What tends to happen, of course, is that we get caught up in agreeing and disagreeing. Something strikes a chord and our mind takes off in a new direction. We're still taking in words, but we are not really reading. The practice is to notice when that is happening, then – quite naturally – come back to the reading.

It is the same with listening, which in many ways is a lost art. In many Buddhist monasteries and practice centers, students sit in the meditation posture when the teacher is giving a talk. That isn't simply a matter of discipline or uniformity. It is also the best way to listen. You sit with mindfulness, as you would during a meditation period, but now the object of contemplation is the talk. When you find yourself drifting away, you come back to the act of listening.

Listening to a friend isn't any different. Often we get caught up in reactions and opinions, in formulating our reply, instead of being fully involved in what the other is saying. Not much communication is taking place. If, instead, you give yourself to the listening, you will absorb the nuances of what the other is saying, and your own opinions will arise quite naturally. Such a response is likely to be more adequate to the situation.

Our mind is constantly calculating. We want to get from A to B or, if we are really ambitious, A to Z. This practice is about getting from A to A. It takes an expansive approach to the present moment, experiencing the full range of what is happening.

We tend to think of the present moment as a means to some end. If I just do *this* in moment A, I think, I will be happy in moment B. But in this practice every moment is a means and an end. The point of moment A is just moment A. There is no moment B in which you will be more fulfilled than in moment A. Every moment is absolute truth.

The Buddha's teaching is about awakening, or liberation, and that sounds like a goal. But the only way to get there is fully to be where you are, absolutely present in this moment.

Let's take the case of loneliness, for instance, which often conditions our yearning for intimacy with another. Loneliness becomes the point A from which we want to escape. We hope to get to a better place, preferably calm and peace, possibly even awakening.

In the case of loneliness, we have often set up a barrier between ourselves and others. It might even be our quest for liberation; often human beings seem to interfere with that. We isolate ourselves, then wonder why we feel lonely. The path is not to run out and start hugging everyone but to see, in concrete moments, what is separating us, to come into contact with that barrier. Our emphasis is always on what is happening now.

Let's say you're sitting on your cushion and a feeling that we might call loneliness comes up. That is just a name; the feeling in the moment is raw, completely unique. How do we become intimate with it? The best way – as with vacuuming, as with reading – is to see the ways we aren't intimate with it.

One of the subtlest ways we escape loneliness is by explaining it. We go into elaborate theories to understand our loneliness and thereby find some comfort; people have even written books on the subject. We create a complex theory about humankind's essential condition: existential loneliness. We make it into an intellectual monument.

Another way of escape is to tell the lifelong story of our own loneliness. It's a long tale, deeply moving, and we love it; we tell it to anyone who will listen. If we can't find anyone else, we once again tell it to ourselves. We prefer the story of our loneliness to the present experience because, in the story, the "I" is the center of things. The ego is glad to keep the story alive, as long as it can be the star.

We escape by justifying our loneliness. We might find someone else to blame, always a satisfying strategy. We also deny and repress it, looking for something else – anything! – to give our attention to.

We might in our approach to loneliness have to be patient through a long period of watching ourselves try to run away, hours and days, months and years. Finally the day comes when loneliness surfaces and we don't do any of that. Our mindfulness joins the feeling, and there is no thinking. We're not for or against it. There is just an innocent and naive seeing of it. To understand loneliness we have to commune with it; we have to let it blossom, tell its story – not necessarily in words – and fade away. And one excellent way to do that is with the mindfulness we learn on the meditation cushion.

When people first practice mindfulness, they often have a mistaken understanding of it. They see it as a detachment from experience, a distancing, as if you were up on a hill with binoculars looking down at a battle taking place in a valley. You can see it but you're not really taking part in it. You're relatively safe.

My understanding of mindfulness is that it is not detached at all. It is participant observation. You're not on the mountain but right down in the valley in the midst of the battle, completely awake to what is happening. You surrender to the experience, the same way you might surrender to the breathing or to the feelings in your body, but in this case you're surrendering to the complicated experience of what we call loneliness. You don't cook it with concepts, explanations, or evasions. You just let it be.

How is that different, people often ask, from just being lonely? The difference is in the quality of wakefulness. When you're just feeling lonely, you're lost in it. If the experience is really bad, you might be flattened. But when you practice mindfulness, you're not lost; you're found. You're standing in the midst of your experience and are entirely alive to it.

What you discover when you are able to do that is the law we've already mentioned: Every phenomenon is impermanent. It has a beginning, a middle, and an end. You also find that the energy of mindfulness transforms the experience. It releases an energy that is frozen in loneliness and makes it seem so solid. You begin to see that because your experiences are impermanent, they are all workable. You are able to face all of the productions of the mind.

The end of loneliness comes about through full communion with it. The subject/object dichotomy falls away and we simply *are* loneliness; there is no "I" left to feel sorry for itself. If we can be with loneliness for every moment of its life, if we can allow it to flower and watch it without separation until it disappears, we will learn something about loneliness and about life.

Something is missing that makes that communion possible. That something is the *me,* the *mine* of it. It is the identifying of loneliness as mine that prevents the opening. In clear seeing we leave me and mine behind. There is just the loneliness.

When loneliness is digested in this way, we come upon aloneness, which is a very different matter. You happen to be alone but you're connected to everything.

But we can't turn emptiness of self into another goal, one more accomplishment. There is an old Jewish joke about that. It was a high holy day in the synagogue, and the rabbi came in and spoke to the congregation. "You think of me as your rabbi, your leader, you think of me as a holy man, but I want you to know I'm nothing, I'm nobody. There's nothing here." He pounded his breast in emphasis. The congregation was stunned at his show of modesty.

The assistant rabbi stood up and got into the act. "You think *he's* nothing? *I'm* nothing. *I'm* nobody. I'm even less than he is." Again the congregation was deeply moved. These were men whom they normally put on a pedestal.

Finally, in the back, the janitor stood up in his work clothes. "I'm nothing! I'm no one! I'm less than the dust I sweep off the floor."

The rabbi shook his head, turning to his assistant in disgust. "Look who thinks he's a nobody," he said.

The practice of intimacy can have a number of ramifications in your life, some major, some not so major. Years ago I was teaching in Cambridge at a moment when French food was in fashion. This was long before croissants were showing up at fast-food restaurants. Eating a croissant – or even knowing how to pronounce the word – gave one an air of sophistication. I was teaching this practice of intimacy, of being with the rawness of your experience, and a student came in one day and told me she had just realized she didn't like Brie. She'd been eating it for years but that day had been intimate with the experience. She'd spent all that time eating a concept.

I had somewhat the opposite experience when I went to Korea. I had been studying with Zen master Seung Sahn for some time, and he finally took me and two other students to his native country. I didn't like the food at all. It seemed extremely monotonous, just rice and pickled vegetables. I was a Jew from Brooklyn, and they didn't serve coffee and cake. It particularly irked me that they had no concept of breakfast. They ate the same food in the morning as at other meals.

We Americans made a number of jokes about the food, as a way of distancing ourselves from the experience. I was the ringleader. One day my teacher exploded. He literally stood me against a wall and shouted, "Where are you?"

"Korea," I said.

"Exactly," he said.

He meant: *Be* in Korea.

When I finally began to do that, when I quit expecting

something else and just ate what was there, I found I actually liked the food. Today Korean is one of my favorite cuisines.

A more poignant example came up toward the end of my father's life, when he was in a special home with Alzheimer's. For the first six months I had a great deal of trouble visiting him. I was comparing him with the way he had been before, clear thinking, intelligent, extremely astute. That image kept coming between us. Furthermore, I had done a large amount of reading on his condition and had a complicated image of what it involved. I kept seeing him as an Alzheimer's patient instead of my old, badly wounded, and lovable father.

Finally I realized what I was doing. I wasn't being with him. We were separated by a diagnostic category.

My subsequent visits were still difficult. But before, there had been a certain sameness to them. Now I saw him as he actually was, on that particular day. And when I looked closely, I saw there was more going on than I'd imagined. He actually seemed happy sometimes. I checked with the nurses and aides who took care of him, and they agreed. Dropping the diagnostic category enabled me to join him in his own kind of humor, even though it made no sense to me. Who says you have to understand somebody's words before you can laugh with him?

The kind of intimacy I'm talking about is not just available in extraordinary circumstances. The place to cultivate it is in the simplest things. When you follow the breathing, see it just as it is. When a bird sings outside, just hear the sound. When you walk, feel your feet touch the ground. Taste your food as you eat. Then, when you have a more complicated state to be intimate with – like aging, sickness, or death – it won't seem so formidable. You can do it in the same direct, natural, and simple way.

THE DEPTH OF THE MOMENT

Most people, of course, connect the word *intimacy* with relationship, and all of these principles apply in that realm as well. I remember reading some years ago in a book by psychiatrist R. D. Laing about a man who could function sexually with his wife only when he had the image of another woman in his mind; that would certainly be a failure of intimacy. But it would be the same thing if he had an image of his wife in his mind, some memory of past lovemaking, instead of being with her as she was in the present.

Often in relationship that is what we do. We are relating to an image we have of the other – an accumulation of past actions – rather than to the real person in the vibrant present. Often both partners are holding an image, so that an image is relating to an image. How can that be intimate? Instead we should see our partner with today's eyes, as if he or she were a totally new creation in every moment. That is what keeps a relationship alive.

People sometimes wonder if this practice of being intimate with experience requires a great deal of energy. Most of us drift mindlessly through life, and this practice of mindfulness sounds exhausting. Actually, quite the opposite is true. You will find, as you begin noticing your body and mind, that you use a great deal of energy in your habitual running away from things, avoiding and repressing them. If all that squandered energy is brought into the service of seeing what we are averse to, we discover that the mind is capable of immense power and focus. It can stand up even to the fears of sickness, aging, and death.

People also get the feeling that the practice is fatalistic. We keep saying, Be with things as they are, as if the point is to sit and be with loneliness all your life. Or you're on retreat and the building catches on fire, with flames leaping through the roof, and you imagine that the perfect meditator would be sitting there mindful of being warm, mindful of being extremely warm, mindful of feeling his flesh start to burn. . . .

The kind of clear seeing I'm talking about is more intelligent, not less so. The perfect meditator would be the first one out of the building. He'd be the first to smell the smoke and warn everyone else.

And adopting this practice doesn't mean you'll spend the rest of your life staring at loneliness. It means you'll have a choice. Most people – without knowing it – are slaves to mind-states like loneliness and fear. They spend their whole lives feeling assaulted by them. Once you discover these mind-states are workable, you won't have to let them push you around.

It is likely, though, that the deeper you get into this practice, the more you'll choose simplicity. You won't need to be entertained and occupied all the time. You'll find that your everyday experience – which you had tended to overlook – is extremely rich.

When you go out into nature, for instance, you can approach it in complete innocence: Can trees, rocks, and flowers teach us anything? Can we meet them with no ideas, stand in front of them with complete openness and see what is there? Similarly, when we listen to music, we tend to have all kinds of associations: I remember the first time I heard this piece; it really reflects the composer's biography; this interpretation isn't as good as some others I've heard. The question is: Can you hear it as pure sound, just follow it the way you follow the breathing, with no interpretation at all? That experience is much different.

One place where the Buddha directly addressed these teachings on intimacy was in the *Sutra on the Love of Ideal Solitude,* in which he advises us not to cling to the past or lose ourselves in the future, since the past is no longer and the future is not yet. That doesn't mean thoughts of the past don't arise; rather, we're not enslaved or attached to them. Thoughts of the future also arise, but we are not burdened by them or lost in daydreaming about them.

It is also possible to be – as the Buddha says – swept away by the present. That takes place when we identify with something that is happening in our body or our mind, when we see it as *me* or *mine*. We are then as lost in the present as if we were in the past or future.

It isn't thoughts themselves that are the problem but how we relate to them. I once had a student in an introductory practice group who took to insight meditation right away but was quite unhappy when the group was over. I asked him why, and he said he didn't see how he could continue, because he worked as a city planner and always had to be thinking about the future. But obviously, certain kinds of planning for the future are important for our lives and can be very much a part of practice, when we are grounded in the present and aware that what we are doing is planning.

Similarly, I have had a number of students who are writers, who deal with incidents from their past, just as I have done throughout this book. It isn't necessarily a problem when thoughts of the past and future come up, just as there is no guarantee we're mindful when we're in the present. It's a question of how we're relating to these mental events.

The Buddha once had a visitor who asked why his monks were so peaceful and radiant. He said that they didn't hanker after the future or try to revive the past but sustained themselves on the present. That idea of sustaining ourselves is the key. The present moment, when approached in the right way, actually gives us nourishment.

The way to find that nourishment is not just to see things as they are but to see with wisdom, to practice mindfulness with discernment. The word in Pali is *satipanna*. You are present with what is happening but you don't identify with it; you're just extremely attentive. If there is a moment's inattention, the "I" is born again, but then you see that and come back to things as they are. The ideal solitude that the Buddha is describing is available even in the midst of a crowd, when the "I" drops away and you are simply open to whatever is happening.

Another way to practice intimacy with the present moment is to reflect on interbeing, the way so many things come together to sustain us. In Japan, where I practiced Zen, meditators acknowledge the fact of interbeing by rituals of bowing. After a sitting, for instance, they bow to their cushion and to the meditator across from them. Because you are here, they are saying, I am able to practice. Seeing other people persevere helps us to meditate. Meditators also bow to statues of the Buddha and to the hall as a whole. They even bow to the toilet.

They could also bow to toilet paper. I sometimes pose a question to my students on a long retreat: Which is more important, the teacher or toilet paper? If I were to disappear for a few days, I think you'd do pretty well. You know how to walk and sit, and you have a schedule to follow. But what if we ran out of toilet paper? That would be a catastrophe.

One of the most beloved and useful teachings in Zen is Dogen's book, *Instructions to the Cook.* He wrote instructions for all of the positions in the monastery, but his instructions to the cook are the most famous because they so directly apply to all of life.

In that book he talks about how he traveled to China as a young man to find a teacher, and just after he arrived he met a cook from one of the monasteries. This sixty-one-year-old man had walked fourteen miles to buy mushrooms for a special soup for the monks and was planning to return immediately. Dogen asked if he couldn't stay instead and let someone else prepare the food, because they had been having a talk about the dharma and he wanted to continue. The cook laughed at such a suggestion. "My good friend from abroad," he said, "you do not understand what practice is all about."

Dogen was acting as if studying the dharma were important

Intimacy with Living and Dying

but cooking food were not, as if the priest in the monastery were important but the cook were not. But in China – and later in the monasteries Dogen set up in Japan – being cook was a high honor; the cook was a senior person of mature practice. Cooking lunch in the kitchen was not considered inferior to sitting in the meditation hall. It was also no less practice.

In the same way, Dogen instructed his cook not to make distinctions in the kitchen. He was to take as much care with a leftover soup of wilted greens as he did with a fine cream soup for visiting dignitaries. Dogen actually said to give the same care to the greens as if they were your own eyeballs. It isn't that old wilted greens are inherently important but that they are your life in that moment. We should give total respect and attention to whatever we're doing.

Sometimes we divide our time into categories; you have time for work, time for exercise, time for eating, time for your partner, time for the children, and finally, you hope, a little time for yourself. But the dharma attitude is that all time is for yourself; whatever you're doing, however trivial, is equally important to everything else. No time is wasted.

One famous Buddhist sutra says that if one mote of dust were removed from the universe, the entire thing would collapse. That is the dharma attitude. Absolutely everything is essential.

Early in my life as a meditator, I had two encounters with death that speak to this practice of intimacy. When I was in Korea and staying at a monastery, one of the nuns died. There was a most impressive ceremony; all of the monks and nuns came together, walking in procession down a hill, and they chanted while the body was cremated. The Zen master I was sitting beside sobbed as the service took place. He was really wailing. I was embarrassed for him.

At the time I had something of an Alan Watts–paperback view of Zen. I imagined that Zen monks were serene and encountered every experience with a perfect calm. So I was troubled by that scene at the funeral; I asked for an interview with the monk who had been wailing and brought it up with him. He roared with laughter. He had entered the monastery at the same time as the nun, he explained, and he'd known her for years. He would miss her. He'd felt a deep sorrow at her funeral, had expressed it fully, and was done with it.

Some years later when I was studying with Ajaan Suwat, he told me he'd been extremely close to his teacher. Especially when he'd been younger, he had wondered how it would be when the man died. He had been quite fearful. But his practice deepened, and when his teacher actually did die, he felt complete serenity, along with a deep love. He understood that his teacher had been an impermanent phenomenon like any other and that in dying he'd been following an inevitable law.

That made me wonder about the Korean monk. I told Ajaan Suwat the story, and he listened carefully. At the end he said, "If his understanding had been deeper, he wouldn't have carried on that way."

I'm not sure. If I had to pick, I'd say that the first monk's reaction seemed more authentic. But I don't think of either of these reactions as being superior, as long as they expressed the truth of the moment. The important thing is not to have an ideal about how you handle a situation like grieving. If you're serene, feel serenity. If you're sorrowful, feel that. Both feelings could be perfectly authentic.

In a way this practice is the same for the advanced student as for the rank beginner. All you can do is be true to your experience as it is. Once I was sitting in on an interview at the Cambridge Zen Center and a man came in who was extremely excited, saying he'd just had an enlightenment experience. He described it in great detail. The teacher listened and in the kindest possible way asked, "Can you show me this experience right now?" He was letting the student know that if the experience happened in the past, he didn't really have it anymore. What is important is what is happening now.

We often have the feeling, about one thing or another in our lives: If only this weren't here I would be happy. If only I weren't afraid, or angry, or lonely. If only I didn't have to do the dishes, or take out the trash, or do my income tax. If only I weren't old, if I weren't sick, if I didn't have to die. But those things are here. This is the situation as it is. And none of it keeps you from practicing. None of it really keeps you from being happy. It is what you do with it that makes a difference.

And the thing to do is always the same: Give yourself to it completely. Be intimate.

APPENDIX
Meditation and the Practice of Awareness

The method of meditation I teach can be seen as a two-step process – *samatha* and *vipassana,* or calming and wisdom – with breath awareness as the cornerstone of the practice. The breathing is an ideal object to focus on. It isn't like a mantra; it has no cultural connotations or other associations. It isn't like a physical object, so that you have to be in a certain place or carry it with you. Breathing is simple and portable; we are all doing it all the time. We can notice it not just when we are sitting in meditation but at any time during the day. And it is always happening in the present. It is our doorway into the present moment.

In order to practice breath awareness as a formal method, the meditator chooses a quiet place and settles into a relaxed but erect sitting posture: cross-legged, with a cushion under the buttocks to help the spine stay straight; kneeling, usually with a cushion or a bench under the buttocks for support; or sitting in a chair, with the feet on the floor. In all of these postures there are three points of contact, so you are stable, like a three-legged stool, and you hold yourself straight, not in a rigid military way but in a relaxed manner, with just the amount of energy that it takes to stay erect.

Then you bring your attention to the process of breathing, in whatever locale it seems most vivid to you, the nostrils, the chest area, or the abdomen. You don't try to breathe in some particular way. You simply observe the breathing as it is, the in-breath, perhaps a short pause, the out-breath, perhaps a longer pause. You take notice of this simple process without which none of us would be alive. You don't *do* it; you let it happen. You surrender to the natural process that is already going on.

The act of following the breathing is quite profound; it can be, quite literally, the work of a lifetime. The more we watch it, the more we see that the breath is a whole world, a universe unto itself, and as we follow it over the course of months and years we go deeper and deeper.

Some breaths are long; some are short. Sometimes the breathing seems to take place in the chest; sometimes it is way down in the belly. Sometimes it feels brief and tight and constricted; other times it is effortless and very deep. It might be smooth, like silk, or rough and coarse, like burlap. All of these variations are possible, and countless others in between, even within the space of a single sitting. There is tremendous variety in the simple act of breathing. You realize eventually that no two breaths are alike.

The human mind, of course, is a lively instrument, and it has many things it would like to do other than follow the breathing. Most of us are quite restless and distracted; we don't realize just how distracted until we try to do a simple thing like following the breathing. Our minds, it seems, would rather do anything else. All kinds of things come up. That mental activity isn't really a problem; it's a discovery. You're seeing how wild your mind really is.

But at this stage of the practice, you don't want to look at that wildness in detail. When you see that the mind has wandered away, notice that, then come back – without any feeling of blame or judgment – to the simple act of breathing. At some sittings it may seem that that's all you're doing: noticing you're away, then coming back. Other times – especially as your practice progresses – you may be able to stay with the breathing for longer and longer periods. It doesn't matter how you're doing; this isn't a competition, and you don't want to struggle. Come to see, instead, that the awareness of unawareness is in itself valuable practice. Wandering away from the breathing isn't a mistake or the sign of a weak character. Simply follow the breathing, and when you notice you're away, come back.

The point of *samatha* practice is primarily to calm the mind. But of course, you can't help noticing what is coming up as you do that, and sometimes you will notice that one thing is coming back again and again, maybe a pain in the body, maybe a state of mind, like anger or fear. It is as if this one thing keeps calling you away from the breathing.

Sometimes even in this early stage of the practice it is a good idea to expand the scope of your awareness to include what has become problematic. You can also temporarily drop the breath and give some attention to whatever keeps calling you away. You pay attention to it for a while, the same way you've been focusing on the breathing, and that usually has the effect of calming it down and making it less persistent. Once it has lost some of its charge, you can go back to the breathing.

Beginners often ask how long they should sit. I really have no idea. In the introductory class I teach, which lasts ten weeks, I start people out at about fifteen minutes and try to work up to an hour, under the assumption that, between the weekly classes, they are sitting most days at home. On retreats most of our sittings are forty-five minutes, though some last for an hour. I encourage newcomers to sit a bit beyond what they regard as their limit, to challenge themselves without making sitting an ordeal. If there is no challenge they lose interest; if the challenge is too severe they may get discouraged and stop practice.

But however long you sit, the end of the sitting period should-n't mark the end of mindfulness. The real point of practice is to bring the same kind of attention to everything; just as you give your attention to the breathing as you sit, you should give your attention to taking a shower, eating breakfast, talking to your family. Sitting and following the breathing, because it is so sim-ple, is in some ways the easiest thing we do. Our real goal is to be as mindful as possible in all the activities that make up our day.

People also ask how long they should follow this first step of practice before they go on to the second. That is another impos-sible question. What I usually say is that you should continue fol-lowing the breathing until you get reasonably good at it, until you achieve some degree of calm and stability. That doesn't mean that other things don't come up but that you're able to notice them fairly quickly and come back to the breathing. Thoughts may still be there, but you're able to let them come and go without getting caught up in them.

In a ten-week introductory class, I might move on to the sec-ond step after seven or eight weeks. On a nine-day retreat, at which people are meditating all day, I move on after three or four days. I always let people know that they don't have to switch. If they want to continue with the breathing, that is perfectly all right.

Following the breathing is not kindergarten. It really is, as I've said, a profound practice, which gets more profound the more you do it. You shouldn't feel any compulsion to move on. Conscious breathing can help take you all the way to enlightenment.

The second step opens to a much larger field. Ultimately it opens to a kind of attention that is limitless, literally infinite. In this style of meditation, you might begin a sitting by focusing on the breathing, but once you have achieved some degree of calm you open the attention to whatever is happening, in your body and your mind and your surroundings. You might retain the breathing as a kind of anchor; that is probably a good idea for most people, though some will drop the breath altogether.

Now you are opening to the things you saw as distractions before, all the phenomena that were taking you away from the breathing. Before, they were in the background and the breathing in the foreground. Now, perhaps, they are the foreground and the breathing is the background. Or perhaps – as the practice grows more subtle – there is no foreground or background; there is just everything that is happening, all at once, a unified field.

There will be sounds, certainly; almost anywhere you are, even in a supposedly silent meditation hall, there are sounds, both inside and outside the room. There might be sensations in the body: a feeling of pain or tension, one of relaxation or relief. There might be smells, or a breeze passing through. There might be thoughts. You don't – as when you were following the breath – want to get caught up in a process of thinking, but you will certainly see thoughts pass through your mind. There might also be complex emotional states like fear or sadness, composed of both thoughts in the mind and feelings in the body.

Watching all of these phenomena come and go is more complicated than following the breathing; watching the breathing has prepared you for this more complex practice. Sometimes it may seem too complex; too many things are present, or you keep getting lost in thought. In that case it is probably a good idea to go back to the breathing, perhaps for a few breaths, until you've calmed down, or perhaps for the remainder of the sitting. That isn't an admission of defeat. It is just wisdom: seeing how things are for you and what the best way to practice is.

In another way, of course, what I'm describing isn't complicated or difficult at all. What you are really learning – and this begins with following the breath – is the art of doing less and less until finally you are doing nothing, just being as you are and letting your experience come to you. There are no distractions; you are mindful of your present experience just as it is. Nothing in particular is supposed to happen. You attend to what is there just because it is there. It is your life at that moment. We are used to doing things all the time, trying to change our environment, improve our situation, so it may seem difficult to do nothing. Actually, there is nothing easier. You just sit and let the world come to you.

In time you will see that these two steps – *shamatha* and *vipassana* – are not easy and difficult, or basic and advanced; they are just two ways to practice, one of which is appropriate for some times, one for others. You'll begin to see it as an art, moving from the breath to a wider focus or – sometimes – deciding to go back to the breath again. *Samatha* and *vipassana* work together like the right and the left hand in cooperation. A calm steady mind is more able to see insightfully. And insights calm the mind. There is not necessarily a right way to move back and forth, certainly not a perfect way. This isn't a realm where perfection is possible. You never come to the end of the practice of awareness. It will serve you well for the rest of your life.

GLOSSARY

All terms are in Pali unless otherwise noted.

ANAPANASATI   Mindfulness with breathing.

ANUSAYA   Underlying, latent disposition or tendency of mind.

ASUBHA   Contemplation of the unloveliness of the body.

BHIKKHU   Meditator, monk.

DHARMA   (Sanksrit; Pali: *Dhamma*) Natural law or teaching of the Buddha.

DUKKHA VEDANA   Unpleasant, painful sensations.

KARMA   (Sanskrit; Pali; *Kamma*) Intentional action.

KILESA   A torment of mind.

MARANASATI   Mindfulness of death.

PASADA   Clarity and serene confidence.

SAMADHI   Concentration.

SAMATHA   Serenity.

SATI   Mindfulness.

SATIPANNA   Mindfulness with discernment.

SATIPATTHANA   Establishing mindfulness.

SAMVEGA   An anxious sense of the urgency of dharma practice.

SUTTA   Discourse of the Buddha.

VIPASSANA   Insight, wisdom.

YOGI   Meditator.

YONISO MANASIKARO   Wise attention, careful consideration.

BIBLIOGRAPHY

Chah, Ajaan. *Our Real Home*, Bodhi Leaves, no. B111. Kandy, Sri Lanka: Buddhist Publication Society, 1987.

Goenka, S. N. "What Happens at Death?" *Sayagyi U Ba Khin Journal*. Igatpuri, India: Vipassana Research Institute, 1994.

Kapleau, Philip. *The Zen of Living and Dying*. Boston: Shambhala Publications, 1998.

Krishnamurti, J. *On Living and Dying*. San Francisco: Harper San Francisco, 1992.

Longaker, Christine. *Facing Death and Finding Hope*. New York: Doubleday, 1997.

Maha Boowa, Ajaan. "Feelings of Pain" and "Investigating Pain." In *Straight from the Heart*. Udorn Thani, Thailand: Wat Pa Baan Taad, 1987.

Mullin, Glenn H. *Living in the Face of Death*. Ithaca, N.Y.: Snow Lion Publications, 1998.

Nanayon, Upasika Kee. "A Good Dose of Dhamma for Meditators When They Are Ill." In *An Unentangled Knowing*. Kandy, Sri Lanka: Buddhist Publication Society, 1996.

Rinpoche, Sogyal. *The Tibetan Book of Living and Dying*. San Francisco: Harper San Francisco, 1992.

Rosenberg, Larry. *Breath by Breath*. Boston: Shambhala Publications, 1999.

Silananda, U. *The Four Foundations of Mindfulness.* Boston: Wisdom Publications, 1990.

Smith, Rodney. *Lessons from the Dying.* Boston: Wisdom Publications, 1998.

Thanissaro, Bhikkhu. "Beyond Coping," available from Access to Insight: Readings in Theravada Buddhism, at *www.accesstoinsight.org.*

RESOURCES

For further information regarding Insight Meditation, please contact one of the following practice centers:

Abhayagiri Monastery
16201 Tomki Road
Redwood Valley, CA 95470
(707) 485-1630

Barre Center for Buddhist Studies
149 Lockwood Road
Barre, MA 01005
(978) 355-2347

Bhavana Society
Route 1, Box 218-3
High View, WV 26808
(304) 856-2111

Cambridge Insight Meditation Center
331 Broadway
Cambridge, MA 02139
(617) 441-9038

Insight Meditation Society
1230 Pleasant Street
Barre, MA 01005
(978) 355-4646

Metta Forest Monastery
P. O. Box 1409
Valley Center, CA 92082
(619) 988-3474

Spirit Rock Meditation Center
P. O. Box 909
5000 Sir Francis Drake Boulevard
Woodacre, CA 94973
(415) 488-0164

Audio tapes of talks by Larry Rosenberg and other Insight Meditation teachers are available from:

Dharma Seed Tape Library
Box 66
Wendell Depot, MA 01380
(978) 544-8912